D1571893

EMMA PATERSON

EMMA PATERSON

She Led Woman Into a Man's World

by Harold Goldman

1974
LAWRENCE AND WISHART
LONDON

ISBN 0 85315 3051

Printed in Great Britain by
The Camelot Press Ltd, Southampton

Contents

Acknowledgments

A great many people including librarians, colleagues and friends have helped me during the six years I have been collecting material about Emma Paterson.

To many I give my general thanks but I must mention a few by name: My son, David Goldman, for the painstaking research without which I could not have written half as much; Henry Fry who persisted and encouraged until the work was complete; Margaret Godwin who typed and re-typed from bad writing without a sign of impatience; librarians at the British Museum, Chelsea, Holborn, Victoria, Westminster, the General and Municipal Workers' Union research department, Marx Memorial Library, Fawcett Library, St. Bride Printing Library and The National Society (CE) for promoting Religious Education, and many others.

TO MABEL

Foreword

by

LEN MURRAY

General Secretary of the Trades Union Congress

Trade Unionists will be grateful to Harold Goldman for reminding us how much we all owe to the pioneers of trade unionism. His account of the life and times of Emma Paterson is a tribute long overdue to a woman to whom the Webbs referred in their *History of Trade Unionism* as "the real pioneer of modern women's trade unions" and G. D. H. Cole described as "the only early feminist who had any knowledge of trade union problems". It is fitting that this book should be published in the year which marks the Centenary of Emma Paterson's formation, in July 1874, of the Women's Protective and Provident League. This was not itself a trade union but its main object was to promote trade union membership among women.

The main reason why I welcome the opportunity of writing this Foreword is because of Emma Paterson's close association with the Trades Union Congress itself. She was one of the first two women delegates to the eighth Congress in 1875 in Glasgow, but she was not unknown because the previous Congress had received a letter in which she called attention to the need to extend trade union membership among women to ensure "a fair day's pay for a fair day's work". She became a regular delegate to Congress and in the year of her death in 1886 she was

9

the first woman to stand for election to the Parliamentary Committee (the forerunner of the present General Council), and was by no means bottom of the poll. She started a campaign at the 1878 Congress which led to the appointment of women as factory inspectors in 1893.

She could also be said to be the architect of the arrangements to look after women's special interests within the TUC. Her Protective and Provident League became the Women's Trade Union League and the transfer of its work to the TUC in 1921 led to the establishment of our Women's Advisory Committee. The roots of our annual TUC Women's Conference also can be said to go back to 1877 at the Leicester Congress when the League invited delegates to a "women's conference" to discuss women's problems. Emma was careful to explain that this was not because of the refusal of the main Congress to discuss women's problems but because the women considered it "would not be fair to overcrowd the Congress programme". Even so, there were men delegates to Congress who were not sorry to see separate arrangements. She also appreciated the importance of Trades Councils and worked closely with the London Trades Council.

The nineteenth century was the heyday of the middle- or upper-class women with a social conscience who worked unstintingly to further the cause of women, but Emma was the first notable woman leader with a working-class background. She had her feet planted firmly on the ground, and knew at first hand not only the problems of working women but that the only way to solve them was through a strong trade union Movement supported as strongly by women as by men, but, at the same time, she saw no reason why women should lose their identity. Today she would be glad to see the increasing fulfilment of her aim, with 2,500,000 women in unions affiliated to the TUC and going up each year.

Emma Paterson achieved great things in her brief life of thirty-eight years and it was fitting that the TUC should have been officially represented at her funeral by the Secretary of its Parliamentary Committee. One can only speculate on what greater achievements there might have been had she lived a normal span.

March 1974

Prologue

Grave Number 4659

Saturday, May 18, 1968, was a wet day. Henry Fry asked me to go with him to Paddington cemetery in Willesden to photograph the grave of Emma Paterson. I'd never heard of her. My son, David, came with us and on the way Henry, known for his enthusiastic collecting of "visual history" of the Labour movement, explained.

"She founded trade unions for women," said Henry. "She's trade unionism's forgotten woman." Her grave bore out Henry's words. He led us to a mound of overgrown earth with no headstone and no name, only a number— 4659. Henry bent down in the rain as if a closer look at the anonymous square of long grass would somehow bring him closer to an understanding of this person who saw the needs of working women but neglected her own so effectively that she died in 1886, a worn-out old lady at the age of thirty-eight.

At the time of her death there were more than thirty unions for women in the League she founded. They were small, most of them no larger than union branches today, but they represented many trades and had an influence out of proportion to their size.

Emma's husband, Thomas Paterson, is buried in the same grave. A remarkable man, craftsman and scholar, Thomas shared his wife's devotion to the cause of working people and shared, too, her anonymity in their few square feet of earth.

13

Emma and Thomas Paterson were not the first to occupy the plot of ground 6½ ft. long by 2½ ft. wide, the size of a modern single bed, bought by him on April 10, 1875, on the death of his maiden aunt, Lucy Miller.

Thomas was poor and expected to remain poor. But with a touch of Victorian providence, he decided there should at least be a small, secure place for members of his family when they died.

Aunt Lucy was seventy when her time came, and another aunt of Thomas's, Mrs. Mary Walker, joined her four years later.

Thomas followed, into the same plot, in 1882 and Emma in 1886. Two more members of his family were to be buried in the same grave—Thomas's sister Agnes who died in 1900 at seventy-seven and Elizabeth, who lingered on as a patient in Tooting Bec mental hospital until 1920 when she died at eighty-two.

Following the record of Elizabeth's burial there is an entry in the cemetery book: "Grave full."

Emma's obscure and overcrowded resting place, with its six occupants at different levels, bore no clue to the family's identity until a tablet was placed on it by the Trade Union Labour Co-operative History Society, generally known as TULC, of which Henry is secretary.

1

Women Trade Unionists

During her short working life of twenty years Emma Paterson founded unions for women in many industries and broke down the men-only tradition of the Trades Union Congress.

But *The Times* of December 6, 1886, in its substantial but slightly inaccurate obituary—it gives her date of birth as April 1847, a year early—went a bit too far when it wrote: "She induced working women for the first time to adopt trade union principles."

The Grand National Consolidated Trade Union, at least ten years before Emma Paterson was born, was enrolling large numbers of women, with a rule (Rule XX) which declared "Lodges of Industrious Females shall be instituted".

Even earlier, in the 1830s, there was the women's Grand Lodge of Operative Bonnet Makers and the Grand Lodge of the Women of Great Britain and Ireland. The Lodge of Female Tailors was angry at the threat to prohibit women from making waistcoats.

And *The Times* of April 19, 1844, writes of Female Gardeners and Ancient Virgins making riotous demands for an eight-hour day at Oldham. In 1847 a woman's suffrage leaflet, probably the first, was produced by Anne Knight, a Chelmsford Quaker and radical.

As far back as 1819, thirty-six women formed a female Reform Association at Stockport.

15

When Emma Paterson was only two years old a group of working tailors was formed at 34 Castle Street East, W., in London. The street later became known as Eastcastle Street, W., and ran parallel with Oxford Street into Regent Street.

The London Tailors' Association began on February 12, 1850, and was one of a number of associations formed about the same time—they included a Needlewomen's Association and a Ladies' Guild.

None of them lasted long. The members worked hard in a kind of co-operative and earned more than they would have done in the employment of masters. But they lacked the experience of finding markets and, as Charles Kingsley, an early adovcate of co-operatives, warned in a pamphlet written over his pen-name Parson Lot, "It is by securing custom, far more than by gifts or loans of money that we can help the operatives."

The custom was not forthcoming and the dream faded.

In the textile industry women had from the first a strong place in the associations. The Lancashire weavers welcomed women, the men insisting on equality of piece-work pay. The spinners followed, but blotted their book with the preservation of certain kinds of work for men only.

Women in the printing trade, where Emma Paterson was to find early and energetic allies, were led by the formidable young Mary Zugg, a bookbinder like Emma herself, who took a prominent part in the strikes of the 1840s.

In 1845 the potters' union made a special appeal to women —if not to join their union, at least to share their aims in opposing the more intensive exploitation of their labour with the introduction of the new flat-press machine.

Two years before Emma Paterson began her own work in organising women into trade unions, Edinburgh women formed themselves into the Edinburgh Upholsterers' Sewers Society—"the oldest durable union for women only".

In a newspaper report of May 10, 1834, there is an account of a strike by seventy washerwomen in Kensington for higher wages. They were getting 2s. 6d. a day and two half-pints of beer. They demanded 3s. a day and no cut in their beer allowance. "After a considerable time had been occupied in parleying as to terms," goes the report, "the washerwomen gained their point and, after taking copious libations of gin, returned the following day to their tubs as usual."

Emma Paterson, then, was certainly not the first to bring women into trade unions, to form trade unions for women, or to "adopt trade union principles". But she brought to her work the energy, organising power and the sheer doggedness against crushing odds that established her clearly as the pioneer of lasting unions for women and an enduring trade union understanding among women.

Any woman who demanded equal treatment with men in industry was regarded as a freak, and certainly no welcome ally to the vast majority of men. In fact men, rapidly forming themselves into associations, thought they could exclude women from industry—and therefore from the competitive market—by keeping them out of their unions.

Emma Paterson side-stepped this opposition by inducing women to take things into their own hands and organise themselves into active and influential women's unions.

Lady Dilke, a lifelong colleague of Emma Paterson, who took over Emma's work when she died, wrote in 1894: "There is no difficulty in fixing the date of the first beginnings of trade unionism among women or in assigning the credit of its foundation to the right quarter. The date was 1874 and the founder was Emma Paterson, née Smith."

But she added a reservation omitted by *The Times*. "I

am here speaking of purely women's unions, for it must not be forgotten that large unions of men and women had existed for many years in the textile trades of the North of England."

Emma was uncompromisingly for equality of pay and rights for women and it is remarkable that she was able to make a notable impact on the women of her time in the face of massive prejudice and vested interest.

Progress towards the establishment of the dignity of working women was rapid while she lived. It slackened later and, approaching the latter half of the 1970s, we still have far to go.

Hers was a time of intense industrial activity and a striving among working people as understanding spread among them of the miserable role reserved for them in the great drama of trade expansion.

The population of England and Wales was rising spectacularly. In 1811 there were 10,164,000 people in this country. Seventy years later the number had shot up to 25,974,000.

Free trade in the 1840s gave the capitalists and industrialists not only a licence to manufacture unlimited wealth for themselves but, they assumed, entitlement to the slave-like submission of their working people. Britain became not only the "workshop of the world" but also the sweat-shop of the world.

But with the political power of the country overwhelmingly in the hands of the exploiters, workpeople had the numbers and the growing will to make their strength felt.

The craft or skilled workers in small societies banded together to make large, powerful unions—particularly in the engineering and textile industries.

Strikes were called for the shorter working day—for nine hours instead of ten in the building industry.

And into the clamour came the voice of woman—not

shrill and appealing as so often in the past, but confident, firm and unyielding, with a dignity and marshalling of fact and argument that commanded a hearing. And that voice was discovered and trained in the first place by a compelling young woman, Emma Paterson.

2

A School in Belgravia

In 1843, five years before their only child was born, Henry Smith and his wife, formerly Emma Dockerill, left the East Ham school where Henry had been headmaster for five years, to live a very different kind of life in fashionable Belgravia.

At that time the East End was a tough quarter harbouring the criminal elements of London. Henry's new school, St. Peter's National School in Belgrave Street South, catered for poor children; but since they were the children of servants in the big houses or of employees in the Royal Mews, they were probably less independent and more manageable than London's East End urchins.

Children in those days did not have to go to school. If they did it was because their parents could afford to send them or because they were the children of poor but respectable workers who were acceptable to charity schools.

Half the children in the land had no education. Little less than half the men and rather more than half the women could not sign their own names.

If a poor child went to school it was either to a parish school or to one of the establishments of that great pioneering educational institution, the National Society for Promoting Education of the Poor in the Principles of the Established Church.

The society had offices in Broad Sanctuary, Westminster,

and lives on with headquarters near Westminster Abbey, as the National Society (CE) for Promoting Religious Education.

It was founded in 1811 and by the 1840s had schools in many parts of the country. The schools were poor and the teachers ill paid—often masters earned little more than £1 a week and mistresses even less.

Belgrave Street South existed in those days as well as the two present Belgrave Streets—Upper and Lower. Belgrave Street South was the extension of Lower Belgrave Street from Ebury Street to what is now Buckingham Palace Road. It is now part of Lower Belgrave Street.

A builder, John Bennett, was the occupier of No. 12 Belgrave Street South and next to him was a "national school" for boys, with Henry Smith as master and Miss Elizabeth King as mistress.

Later, Mr. Bennett's number in the street was given as 15 but, since the national school is still shown next to him, it appears to be a change of street number rather than a move to another building.

Before Henry Smith died of typhoid fever in 1864 the school had been opened for girls as well as boys. The mistress, then Miss Cukow, took charge of the school after the death of Emma's father.

Henry Smith's school was under the jurisdiction of the National Society for Promoting the Education of the Poor in the Principles of the Established Church in England and Wales. From its head office in Broad Sanctuary it administered schools in many parts of London and else-where. If its pupils were poor, the society's servants were in little better fettle, for the rate for schoolmasters in those days was still only £60 a year and for school mistresses £40.

Three years after the Smiths made their home at the school house attached to St. Peter's, the National Society held an inquiry and issued a detailed report on their schools.

Mr. Smith was one of more than 21,000 paid teachers of the society, 12,000 of whom were women. In addition there were some 5,000 assistant masters and monitors who received little payment if any. Salaries during one year amounted to £621,000, making an average of about £30 a year for each teacher. St. Peter's, Pimlico, had 75 boy and 75 girl pupils, and both the classroom and school house were unsecured— this no doubt meant that rent had to be paid.

In the comparatively prosperous area—it came at first under St. George's, Hanover Square—it was estimated that 2,000 children were in need of education. Only a quarter of them were provided for at national schools and another 100 at dame schools, leaving more than 1,000 boys and girls with no education whatever.

A catalogue of equipment for the schools shows that Mr. Smith could, and probably did, order abaci, or arithmetical frames, slates, slate pencils, and quill pens—surely a luxury —in Hamburg red and blue, extra large red, orange or green.

He could not have enjoyed complete relief from the tough life with his East End children, for there is a revealing hint in the specification of desk equipment on offer. This included "cast-iron desk standards, very superior and strong including braces and screws—per pair 7s."

In 1864 the area was ceded to St. Peter's, Eaton Square. Henry Smith spent the rest of the twenty-one years left of his life in this post and it was at the school house in Belgrave Street South that Emma Ann was born on April 5, 1848, and was named after her mother.

It is unlikely that Emma became a pupil at the school, for the education, while basically sound, was limited. Working people had some interest in reading but many had little sustained use for writing. Mr. Smith certainly

22

took Emma's education in hand himself, privately. On the other hand, at quite an early age, Emma helped her father teach. Assistant teachers and monitors were in great demand. Under the "Madras" system children as young as seven became unpaid "assistant teachers" with a class to command.

Young Emma led a happy family life. A particularly close relationship grew between father and daughter. Henry determined that his daughter should have the best education he could give her and encouraged her naturally studious bent. Her cousins and friends made gentle fun of her love of reading, referring to her as "the bookworm".

She was calm, self-possessed and developed considerable charm. Certainly there was nothing stuffy about her. She filled the house with song, and her father was proud not only of the way she studied but also of her skill as a whistler.

"She can whistle as well as any boy," Henry told a friend.

Under his guidance she mastered German and Italian. And for a time she was apprenticed to a bookbinder—a fact which at a later stage in her life enabled her to refer to herself as a "working woman". And it helped her considerably in later years in her approach to trade-union printers.

Her mother was a hardworking person who, until her death, kept close to her daughter. In later years, frail though she was, she laboured to lighten the burden of public work which Emma never refused nor sought to shed.

Emma grew into a quietly determined young woman, at ease in any company and particularly sensitive to the needs of working people. While still in her teens she looked round for a job that would have some meaning and would bring her into contact with ordinary people.

When she was sixteen her father died of typhoid fever. This was a shattering blow to the young girl, who adored him. But it was also a financial disaster.

Henry Smith had been a good headmaster but, like most

23

people close to Emma, and like herself too, he was no hand at making money. He left his wife and his daughter in poverty.

Mrs. Paterson decided to open a school. When this failed she tried again with the help of her well-qualified daughter. But they both lacked business ability and the second venture came to grief too.

Emma now tried teaching outside. She found a job as a governess. It is not difficult to visualise the kind of problems that arose.

This proud, independent-minded young woman, used to speaking her mind in any one of three languages, would be more than a match for an arrogant or demanding employer who crossed her path. Emma was not governess material and before long she was looking round again.

In 1866 she became secretary to an elderly woman employed by the secretary of the Working Men's Club and Institute Union. This was more to her taste and temperament. Her interest was at once engaged and so began an association with working people which continued to the end of her life.

Emma read widely and studied the work of the Union so successfully that, on the recommendation of the woman who employed her and the knowledge of the Union she had absorbed, she was offered the post of assistant secretary to the Union itself. In July 1867, she took up her new appointment. She was then still only nineteen.

The appointment is recorded in the Union's official history:

"Miss Smith is engaged as assistant secretary. But it is found that Connelly Peyton, appointed as a collector in 1866, is a scoundrel who, with duplicate receipt book, has robbed the Union of £130. He is duly prosecuted and convicted and this adds a lawyer's bill of £26 to the loss."

The appointment of a young woman as assistant secretary

was clearly accompanied by some doubts as to whether the Union could afford the luxury.

To Emma, on the other hand, the new work was an unqualified joy.

The Union, like so many "working class" institutions of the day, was a product of middle-class efforts to make the working class more virtuous.

The intention was to keep men out of the public houses, and the clubs began on a temperance basis.

Members later objected to this and were soon running the clubs in their own way with refreshments, billiards, bagatelle, chess and other, less virtuous, pursuits. There were rooms for holding debates and libraries. The clubs spread in time to major towns and then became established throughout the country.

One man alone in those early times brought into the higher administration of the club a breath of the working class.

Thomas Paterson is referred to in the club's fourth annual report in 1866 and later he is mentioned in a pamphlet about the organisation as "Thomas Paterson, a working man member of the council".

He was a cabinet maker and probably the first working class man to get on to the club's council.

The founder was the Rev. Henry Solly, later editor of the *Beehive*, and its first president was Lord Brougham, supported by Lord Lyttelton, the Earl of Rosebery, John Ruskin, the Duke of Argyle, Charles Darwin and others.

If the upper crust ran the clubs, the members were mostly working men who went there, in the first instance, for education.

Membership was open to all political shades but a healthy political outlook developed, as the following extract from a newspaper report in 1877 shows:

"At the Manchester court the secretary of the Rochdale
Working Men's Club brought an action against a railway
company for a breach of contract.

"It seems that in August last members of the club made
an excursion to London, engaging a special train for the
purpose. They arrived safely, but on reaching Kings Cross
station to go home, they found their carriage had been
attached to another 'special' which had been chartered
by a party of conservatives from Rochdale.

Their political sentiments were too strong to allow them
(the club members) to travel by the same train as their
opponents. So they marched off in high dudgeon to St.
Pancras and paid for their journey home."

The action, which the men lost, brought the editorial
reproof that, with all the dangers of travelling by train,
"surely in the case of a railway journey we should be disposed
to make peace with all men".

This independent spirit was a product of the men who
pioneered the clubs and among them was the uncompromising champion of the working class, Thomas Paterson.

The Working Men's Club and Institute Union, in
1862, threads in and out of Emma's story. Thomas Paterson who helped shape it from its earliest days later became
its honorary secretary. After Emma's death a fund founded
in her memory linked the Women's Trade Union League,
a later name for Emma's Women's Protective and Provident
League, with this workmen's organisation.

And, at the club headquarters, Emma worked for the
three joint honorary secretaries of the Union—Hodgson
Pratt, the Hon. Auberon Herbert and Thomas Paterson.
She formed a lasting friendship with the first two and married
the third.

Her five years with the club union were a valuable period

of education and character building for this sensitive but unsentimental young woman.

She was always courteous and direct and she won the respect of the mixed company of working-men members and middle-class organisers.

It took courage in those days for a middle-class young lady with a professional background to mix, even on business terms, with working men. It was regarded as inappropriate, if not downright improper, by the respectable—rather like a present-day Tory minister's daughter going to work among drug-blighted down-and-outs.

An unnamed friend wrote of her at the time:

"There was a cheerful and equable presence of mind and self respect, which made her relations with men perfectly easy both for them and for herself. It would have been impossible for any man to make her a personal compliment, or to be rude."

Her memory for names, dates and facts were noted and the thoroughness with which she tackled every task she was given.

These were the formative years of her life. The experience gave her the appetite for wider and more effective work in the movement for the new freedom people spoke of. Among these, at the top of her list, was the desire for equality for women.

Emma, now a forthright and capable woman of twenty-four, resigned from the Working Men's Club and Institution Union to become secretary of the Women's Suffrage Association. The Union presented her with an illuminated address and a gold watch. They must have been distressed to lose her—and for Emma it proved to be an unhappy move.

27

Her "practical ability and good judgment", as the address put it, were not enough for the suffragettes.

They wanted fire and thunder and while the Association later said she "fulfilled the duties of her office with great zeal and ability", there was a hint in that phraseology of something wanting.

Again we catch the sense of a lacking "quality" in her own reference to her pre-suffragette life as the time "before I was an agitator". She must have regretted leaving that life, because Emma certainly was no natural agitator. She won people by her tact and quiet persuasiveness, and her fist never hit the table.

It could not have surprised her friends that little more than a year later she resigned from the suffragettes. The official reason given was the fact that she and her former chief, Thomas Paterson, had decided to marry. But Emma's friend and colleague in later days, Emilia Pattison, who became Lady Dilke, revealed three years after Emma's death that she was sacked from the Suffragette Society.

"I went to the office of the Society for the Promotion of Women's Suffrage to see the secretary, Emma Smith," wrote Emilia Pattison in the *Fortnightly Review* of June 1889, "who I heard had been dismissed from her post by the committee. The news I found was true. 'The ladies have complimented me on my zeal,' she said, 'but they say my bodily presence is weak and my speech contemptible. So I must make room for someone who can represent them better.'"

Later, on her return from her tour in the U.S., she worked again with the Women's Suffrage Society, but only for a short time.

Emma married Thomas Paterson on July 24, 1873, not, as might have been expected of the daughter of a school headmaster, in church, but at Holborn Register Office. They both gave their address as 2 Brunswick Row, Holborn. He was described as a cabinet-maker while Emma declared herself simply as a "spinster". Her marriage certificate says, incorrectly, that she was twenty-six. In fact she was twenty-five. Thomas was thirty-nine. Perhaps this is how *The Times* came to make its mistake of a year.

Emma had saved enough money at least to pay her equal share of a trip to America where Thomas was eager to study the trade union movement.

She had come to the view that votes for women was not the only answer to the sufferings of her sex. She believed there was much to learn in America about the organisation of women into "friendly societies". Even before she left Britain she was forming plans to "help themselves, as men have done, by combination".

So she and Thomas set off for a working honeymoon in America.

"I am a working woman myself," she told Emilia Pattison (she had been apprenticed to the bookbinder as a girl), "and my work for this society has brought me into contact with large bodies of women in other trades."

Friendly societies and associations were the euphemisms of the day for trade unions. The Patersons were living in a century which opened with the "combination" of work-people still regarded as a conspiracy, punishable by law, while similar association among employers was common and certainly not subject to the same severities of law as the meeting of workpeople to discuss their pay.

At the end of the eighteenth century more than forty Acts of Parliament still forbade workmen from combining, though there is evidence that many defied the law.

It was not until 1824 that the Combination Laws were repealed, and even after that trade unionists who raised their heads above the ground did so at their peril.

But trade unionism was growing, at least among craftsmen, and women backed their men either with support at home or in the more exposed battlefields of industry. Certainly they suffered side by side, men and women together, and neither sex had the monopoly of courage.

Women, however, were weaker in their organisation—for it was never supposed by men that they could form unions. Emma was convinced they could, and in the twenty years of her active adult life she was able to prove herself right.

3

A Manifesto and a Meeting

The Patersons did not find conditions better in America than over here. Emma was on a fact-seeking trip and she kept her attention on her main objectives. All the same she could hardly ignore the grim truth that the male Americans of that time had little respect for women.

The workingmen's organisation, the Noble Order of the Knights of Labor, founded by Uriah Smith Stephens, a tailor, in 1869, while gaining in influence in America at the time of the Patersons' Atlantic trip, was still, nevertheless, a secret organisation.

"The Revolution," wrote James Oneal in *The Workers in American History*, "had simply bequeathed to the workers, at the beginning of the nineteenth century, the barbarous conspiracy code of England enacted a century or two before." Prosecutions took place in many parts of the United States until the second half of the century when the workers forced the government to make unions legal.

In the 1830s it was estimated that 20,000 women in the main cities of the U.S. were earning $1.25 or less for a 16-hour day. Many banded themselves into short-lived "associations" and "societies". These included the umbrella makers who now made an impression on Emma. She mentioned them particularly on her return to England.

She reported that she had "casually" attended a meeting of this Female Umbrella Makers' Union in New York and was struck by the "success and force" of the women workers banded together to accumulate a sick benefit fund.

The umbrella workers must have made some progress since the 1860s when they were the most exploited group of a scandalously ill-treated sex.

They were among the earliest women's trade unions in the U.S.; a thousand umbrella sewers formed themselves into a union in New York City and Brooklyn in the early 1860s.

Six cents was the usual payment for one umbrella, and girls had to work from six o'clock in the morning until past midnight to make twelve umbrellas. Out of this money they bought their own thread.

In October 1863 the women struck for an extra two cents an umbrella, but the organisation was too weak and the strike failed.

Emma certainly found sweated conditions in the U.S. textile industry as wicked as any she saw in Britain. An investigation, concluded shortly before the Patersons arrived in America, showed that shops were "located on the upper floors and were packed so densely that the girls could scarcely move from their chairs; that they had no ventilation except from windows at one end of the rooms, and many of the windows could not be opened. Over half the shops had no toilet facilities and no drinking water."

These women workers earned $1.50 a week. On piece-work they got 25 cents a garment and "the most they could make was two per day". Many averaged six to eight garments a week.

They worked on an average ten hours a day at the shops and, the earnings being so low, they took work home to continue for two or three hours at night.

Some lived three to six to a room in boarding houses, suffering privation and often near starvation.

The Knights of Labor tried to organise the women but met with no real success until some years after the Paterson's visit.

Emma must have found much to ponder in New York. She may well have thought the few somewhat feeble societies she saw worth emulating on her return to England. It is equally certain that she was spurred to organise women in Britain by the determination that they should not continue to suffer as they were suffering on the other side of the Atlantic.

When she returned from the United States, she was impatient for action. She had formed a clear plan of what she must do and she put these ideas forward in an article in the *Labour News* of April 1874.* This is a manifesto for women that must certainly rank among the historic documents of the century. Its impact was immediate, for it led to a conference to discuss its proposals and a committee to implement them.

Emma, no publicity seeker for herself, was well able to ensure a hearing for her plans. She made public speeches on the lines of her manifesto which she circulated privately to people she supposed would be impressed and take action. She gave it the title, "The position of working women and how to improve it".

Her *Labour News* article insisted that the rate of wages paid to women in many occupations was "disgracefully low". She quoted a case at the time fresh in people's memories of a woman working in a lead factory in London. The factory was three or four miles from the woman's lodging and since the woman was earning only 9s. a week for a twelve-hour day she had to walk to and from work, and on too little food to keep her alive. She died leaving three children, and Emma's contention was that other women too were being worked and starved to death and that this

* Full article in Appendix.

particular woman's tragedy came to light only because "she died leaving the children unprotected. Had she supported herself only," Emma went on, "the facts might never have been known."

Women, she wrote, were frequently paid a half or less than half as much as men for doing work as well and as quickly.

She quoted a manufacturer, reported in *The Times* of March 27 of that year. "Skilled women whose labour required delicacy of touch, the result of long training as well as thoughtfulness, received from 11*s*. to 16*s*. or 17*s*. a week, whilst the roughest unskilled labour of a man was worth at least 18*s*."

She was strong in her conviction that legislation to protect women was not in the interests of women. In this she did not always have the support of her friends, and she had, at times, to hold her fire, but she never changed her opinion on the need for women to fight their own battles and not to accept the suspect benevolence of politicians.

The name Emma suggested for her new organisation was the National Protective and Benefit Union of Working Women. Branches would be formed of not less than twelve women. Rules for the collection of subscriptions and the keeping of books followed.

The main object in view, she explained, was to accustom women to the idea of union.

She listed four trades in England and Wales where women were prominent—tailoresses with 38,021 women workers; earthenware with 15,953; straw plain manufacturers with 45,270; and bookbinders 7,557.

She brought in her American experience, speaking of "some very successful unions (in New York) consisting of, and managed entirely by, working women. Two of the largest are the Parasol and Umbrella-makers Union and the Women's Typographical Union."

By way of encouragement of what might be done here among "isolated" classes of people, she cited the agricultural labourers among whom a movement began only three years before and had already developed into a powerful society of 150,000 members, many of whom had increased their wages by one-third.

Emma attacked the "common fallacy" that all cheap production was a benefit to the producers. "Does it benefit women or indeed men either, that cigars, for instance, should be made for 4d. per 100, the price paid, according to the *Beehive* newspaper, to some female cigar makers . . . or that jewel cases can be procured at a very small cost?"

There were other benefits, apart from increased wages, that would come to women from the organisation she had in mind, for instance help in times of sickness or temporary depression in trade. "Women have suffered deeply for want of such assistance."

She gave as an example the distress among women "at a time of great slackness of trade among bookbinders in 1871". This was caused by delay in passing the revised prayer-book through the House of Commons.

According to Emma, during sixteen months two of the men's unions paid out £2,500 in relief to unemployed members. The women in the trade, not being members of the union, had no relief and suffered the greatest distress.

On the other hand, says Emma, the Female Umbrella-makers Union of New York had paid in sick benefits alone, during the three years of its existence, over 1,000 dollars or at the time, £200. "One widow," says Emma, "was supported entirely by the union during an illness lasting two years."

Another form of protection was the guarding against fraudulent claims by employers that work was badly done and would therefore not be paid for, knowing full well that women were quite unable to afford to press a claim for payment.

This declaration of Emma's ends with a plea that was heard—she made quite sure it would be:

"The writer earnestly begs of persons interested in improving the social condition of women to communicate with her with a view to action in this matter, and especially invites information and suggestions from women engaged in trades."

She attached her name and address: Emma A. Paterson (April 1874), 2 Brunswick Row, Queen Square, Bloomsbury, W.C.

And to that address came offers of help from people who remained her working associates for the rest of her short life.

Following her campaign—today it would be called a softening-up operation—by private correspondence, button-holing anyone who would listen (and most people would listen to Emma), writing articles and holding informal meetings, Emma decided that the time was ripe for a full London conference of influential people.

She stated the purpose of the conference simply and directly: it was to form a national union for improving the position of working women.

It was a cheerful young woman full of confidence and sense of purpose who left 2 Brunswick Row, Bloomsbury, on July 8, 1874, for the Quebec Institute in Lower Seymour Street, near Marble Arch, where a fateful meeting was to be held.

In the chair was Hodgson Pratt, her husband's colleague and friend from the Working Men's Club and Institute Union.

Emma's theme at the meeting was based on the paper she

had already circulated. As an example of the disgracefully low wages paid to women in many industries she quoted a case from *The Times*, which showed that skilled women, whose delicate work in a factory was the result of long training, were getting between 11s. and 17s. a week, while unskilled men were taking 18s. a week.

She did not blame the employers alone. Many would give their women workers a fair wage, but while women were prepared to work for a third or a quarter of what they should have, unscrupulous employers would pay them no more and would undersell fair employers in the market.

The remedy was organisation of the women into unions.

Another consequence of underpaid women workers was the hostility this engendered in men.

"The fear that the employment of women will lower their wages has led men to pass rules in many of their trade societies positively forbidding their members to work with women."

At this early stage Emma produced the strange argument which led to trouble and lost her support. She spoke now of a Bill before Parliament to limit the hours of women's work in factories and workshops. "This Bill," she said, "is intended to apply also to children, with whom working women are classed, thus conveying and endeavouring to perpetuate the idea that women are entirely unable to protect themselves, a position, to a certain extent, degraded and injurious."

She saw such legislation as a threat to her main argument that women must look after themselves, strongly organised into unions which demanded equality in all respects with men.

Women "urgently need the protection afforded by combination". If the proposed restrictions became law, "further

37

legislation in the same direction may be proposed, and at present the women affected by it have no means of making known their collective opinion on the subject".

One cannot help wondering if the poor woman in Emma's story of the white lead factory would not have preferred a morsel of selective legislation while she waited for massive women's unions to arise.

To be fair to Emma it should be said that she feared that Acts restricting women's hours would also be used still further to reduce women's earnings or even to exclude women from work altogether. But since sweat-shop employers paid little regard to the most basic needs of women, the first-aid of Parliamentary Acts, however wrongly motivated, was surely not to be sneezed at.

Now Emma aimed a broadside at the Trades Union Congress which had been going along happily for six years without the benefit of women. (Emma was soon to alter that.)

"At three successive annual congresses of leaders and delegates of trade unions, the need of women's unions has been brought before them, and each time some one present has asserted that women *cannot* form unions. The only ground for this assertion appears to be that women *have not* yet formed unions (her italics). Probably they have not done so because they have not quite seen how to set about it."

She then set out a plan for a general organisation of working women and acknowledged her indebtedness for its form to the National Agricultural Labourers' Union.

The main object, she said, was to accustom women to the idea of union. Emma was, in fact, persuaded to avoid the word union in the title given to the organisation later set up.

This is the way Lady Dilke, writing in the *North American Review* in 1893, recalled what happened.

"When, therefore, Emma Smith came back from the States and called on her friends to support her scheme for helping working women to help themselves, they one and all insisted that the society should be christened in such a wise as would not suggest, to the casual hearer, its true character.

"So it came about that we hit on the title Protective and Provident League. It was not till about four years ago that our friends gathered courage sufficient to substitute the word 'trades-union' for the adjective 'protective'. Since then, indeed, things have gone so fast that 'provident' has followed suit."

In the article Lady Dilke recalls an incident which underlined the necessity for caution.

A meeting was called in the early days to start a "society" in a provincial town. Influential middle-class people were approached and just before the meeting opened, one of Emma's friends announced in triumph that she had captured a well-known academic—a professor of logic.

He arrived in person and presented a sum of money towards the expenses of the meeting. But by the time Emma ended her introductory speech he was seen to be in a highly explosive state.

He stood up and shouted: "Why, this is trades-unionism! I can have nothing to do with you; you are trying to violate the laws of political economy!"

He demanded his money back and stormed out of the hall. So much for the professor's logic.

So her original idea, to call her organisation the National Protective and Benefit Union of Working Women, was set aside in favour of the name the Women's Protective and Provident League to which was added the sub-title: "For the formation of protective and benefit societies among women earning their own living". And this led to some misunderstanding of the league's purpose.

First Emma proposed a general union in which women would be classified according to their trades. When enough women in one trade were enrolled to form a separate union, this would be done. She soon abandoned this idea in favour of separate unions from the start.

Emma Paterson's unions for women never gained great strength and many of them had begun to wilt even before her short life ended. It may be that her greatest contribution was the last advantage she quoted as a reason for founding women's separate trade unions. This was "the feeling of strength and mutual sympathy and helpfulness afforded by close association with others".

This feeling she kindled, and it burned ever brighter. She gave women a sense of their importance in industry and an impatience with the assumptions of men. It was not a sex war but rather a firm argument for equal rights as much in the interests of men as of women. Equality is still a live issue, by no means won, but when it comes to be acknowledged, so will the foundations laid by Emma Paterson a hundred years ago.

Emma had no trouble in getting her proposals approved; she had done her groundwork well. They were embodied in a resolution that

1. A committee be appointed, to be entitled the Women's Protective and Provident committee;

2. One of the objects of the association shall be to enable women earning their own livelihood to combine to protect their interests;

40

3. It shall be one of the objects of the association to provide a benefit fund for assistance in sickness and other contingencies;

4. The committee consist of Miss Williams, Miss Downing, Miss Sims, Miss A. Davies, Mr. Hodgson Pratt, Miss Faithful, Miss Wade, Mr. and Mrs. Reed, Miss Sutherland, Mr. S. S. Taylor, Mr. Gale, Mr. Allerdale Grainger, Miss Browne and Mr. and Mrs. Paterson.

Emma was elected secretary and kept the position for twelve years, until her death.

This committee was to change during the early days, for some members found that their other commitments made it difficult to attend meetings. But they were replaced by people like George Shipton and Edith Simcox, who were to play a great part in developing the league during its early days.

Now Emma wasted no time in setting about the formidable task of creating an organisation and getting members.

4

Building a Team

Emma made a few enemies—or, rather, she *had* a few enemies, for she had little capacity for making people dislike her—but she never lost a friend.

The people who came to help her at the beginning of her work in organising women were for the most part far more involved by the time death took her from the work.

Her friendships, however, were the workaday kind. Emma had little time for purely social contacts. She loved her father dearly. When he died she was on terms of intimacy only with her mother and later her husband. Otherwise the sole being which was a friend rather than working comrade was her cat.

On her return from America with her husband, Thomas, she had wasted no time in putting the first stage of a carefully worked-out plan into effect.

She sought out the people whom she knew would help her, and was only concerned with their position in life to the extent that it could further her plans.

She went to those with money, talent, social conscience. She found some among the clergy, and the middle and upper classes, and others she found in the trade union movement.

One of the first persons, and probably the second woman she approached—the first was Eleanor Whyte of the London Bookbinders—eventually left her own mark on the movement.

42

This was the friend with a name strangely similar to Emma's own. Emilia Pattison was a remarkable person— writer, art critic, an outstanding intellectual among the more brilliant people of her day. She was a friend of Ruskin, Robert Browning and George Eliot who is said to have used at least some parts of Mrs. Pattison's character in the drawing of Dorothea Brooke in *Middlemarch*.

Later she became Lady Dilke, wife of Sir Charles Dilke, who would almost certainly have become Prime Minister but for a scandal which ruined his political life.

At the time Emma Paterson sought her help and interest Emilia Pattison was the unhappy wife of Mark Pattison, Rector of Lincoln College, Oxford, whom she had married when she was twenty-one and he was forty-two.

Mrs. Pattison, for all her moving in exalted circles, had a genuine and sincere feeling for working women.

She was active in the suffragettes and gladly turned her energies to the organising of women into trade unions. She was, from its earliest days, a member of the council of the Women's Protective and Provident League. After Emma died she took over leadership of the League and was its president until her death in 1904.

Following her "softening up" campaign in print Emma called her first conference in July 1874. Among those she invited was Canon Kingsley.

Charles Kingsley was the last of the Canons of Middleham, a Yorkshire village still noted for its racehorses as it was in Kingsley's days and indeed a hundred years before. When Kingsley preached there he noted on one occasion eighty horses and their jockeys and grooms crowding the streets on his way to church.

Kingsley is known for his books, less for his political activities. Apart from his novels, which he was driven to write to make good the financial losses he suffered through his political work, he was a prolific writer of tracts and articles exposing the exploitation of working people.

Under the pen-name Parson Lot he fought against the virtual enslavement of needlewomen and slop-workers.

The slop system was a method of contracting and sub-contracting which kept the average earnings of 14,000 women in the clothes trade to little more than 2*s*. a week. Three out of every four garments made came under this system. In his novel *Alton Locke*, Kingsley exposed the sweating system. This book, branded as revolutionary literature in the *Quarterly Review* for September 1851, established even more certainly Kingsley as an inspiration to the young thinkers of his day, than did his article "Cheap Clothes and Nasty" in *Fraser's Magazine*, which, in fact, led him on to writing of the longer work.

In an excellent short book on Kingsley's political work, W. Henry Brown (Co-operative Union, 1924) wrote: "Not only did Kingsley inspire the young men of his day, he also led the young women to recognise their duty and responsibility to their sisters as well as their fellows. Some of his addresses on the problems of health and education were specifically addressed to them, and they were stirred to action by his writings against the sweating system."

When Emma held this first meeting, Kingsley had himself just returned from America where he lectured, opened a House of Representatives session with prayer and met Mark Twain and Longfellow.

But he was near the end of his days. He was ill with pleurisy in San Francisco and he was not a fit man when he went to Emma's conference. The following January (1875) he developed pneumonia and died.

Charles Kingsley could have given Emma Paterson little active help in the early days of her League, but with the high regard in which he was held it was enough that he identified himself with her cause. With other Christian Socialists he had, nearly twenty-five years before, founded the Society for Promoting Working Men's Associations. It was natural that he should now encourage a similar organisation for women.

A footnote should be added to this brief account of Kingsley's part in Emma's campaign. While he wrote tracts and political articles under the pen-name Parson Lot, this conformed with the custom of the time and did not indicate any fear of exposing himself.

Kingsley was courageous. He identified his person openly with his views. He is reported to have stood up at a meeting at which the clergy were under attack and declared "I am a Church of England parson—and a Chartist". This in spite of the fact that he was far more concerned with exposing sweating than promoting Chartism. The Americans, incidentally, thought a great deal of Kingsley; they named five towns after him.

Emma Paterson's plan to form women into their own trade unions met with little more approval in general trade union circles than it did among the employing classes.

However, some of the more far-sighted trade union leaders listened to Emma and then joined her, using their influence in the movement to bring about a change of heart.

George Shipton, founder and secretary of the Amalgamated Society of Housepainters and Decorators, proved himself a great ally.

Shipton had taken over the secretaryship of the London Trades Council two years before from George Odger of the Ladies Shoemakers' Society, a noted orator, who, after ten years as secretary of the trades council, was now devoting more time to the Trades Union Congress where he became a strong supporter of Emma's movement.

The shoemakers had already established their general

welcome to women trade unionists in a resolution to the National Union of Boot and Shoe Operatives' conference in 1872.

This motion said that "all women working at the shoe trade (should) be admitted into the association upon the same terms, and (should be) entitled to the same rights of membership as the men".

It was largely due to the determination of these two far-sighted men, that the TUC in the end took women trade unionists if not to its heart, at least to its councils.

Then there was Henry R. King of the London Book-binders, about whom more will be heard.

Undoubtedly, Emma's greatest encouragement came from the wise council and unwavering support of her husband. Thomas Paterson can be described without any slighting of his abilities which by any standards were immense, as a self-made intellectual.

It was his idea that they should spend their honeymoon in America, and while there he carried out his intention to study the U.S. working-class movement at close quarters.

He was a cabinet-maker by trade and a talented wood-carver, but his main interests in life were the promotion of trade unionism and study.

He was the first genuine working man to join the council of the Working Men's Club and Institute Union. Like many organisations devoted to the uplifting of working people, including Emma Paterson's own Women's Protective and Provident League, it was founded by well-meaning men and women from the upper walks of life.

They were offended by the methods used to defend the way of life they were brought up to expect as their right, and no doubt felt the least they could do was to lessen the gap between their good living and the misery it caused so many of their fellow creatures.

Thomas, a student himself—perhaps it has some significance that he was a Scot—was intensely interested in the education of working men, regarding knowledge as a key to the attainment of justice. He had worked with the union from its early days and had become honorary secretary of the Clerkenwell club.

Once on the council he pressed for the kind of clubs he was convinced were needed—with educational and social facilities.

He clashed on this issue, often bitterly, with the union's founder—in 1862—the Rev. Henry Solly who wanted to spread the clubs and spend their limited resources on publicity and promotion of teetotal clubs.

Thomas Paterson had a strong ally in Hodgson Pratt, honorary director of the union for seventeen years.

Solly eventually resigned and the question of introducing drink and games, the burning question for debate at the time Emma joined the organisation, was settled by popular clamour.

The lighter side of life was coupled with the provision of greater opportunities for study which, because of the national neglect of education, was basic enough.

Thomas Paterson carried for at least the latter fifteen years of his life an ambition to publish the ideas he had formed as a result of his reading and experience. He had little time for this, rather spending the precious hours he could spare from his work in the British Museum reading room with volumes of Berkeley, Kant, Spinoza, Carpenter, Darwin, Lewes and many others, as his wife, Emma, told three years after his death in a preface to the book she published of the manuscripts he left.

The book, *A New Method of Mental Science, with applications to Education and Political Economy,* was published in 1886 by the Women's Printing Society.

47

In it Paterson discussed and compared various theories of existence and put forward his own, which he called "visible thought".

He explained that "mental phenomena are visible and tangible and can be completely differentiated from the physical and may properly be termed metaphysical or hyperphysical". The book, which was unfinished, also contained a fierce attack on Malthus whose theory of population he found "the most complete example of hasty generalisation from an incomplete induction from insufficient facts". He found it difficult to understand "the almost fanatical enthusiasm with which it has been espoused and maintained".

But, as has been seen, Paterson was no mere theorist and he never for a moment, in his pursuit of abstract knowledge, forgot the main purpose of his life.

He was closely engaged in the Workmen's International Exhibition of 1870 at the Agricultural Hall which led to the opening of similar exhibitions all over the country. And he insisted on the publication of the names of workmen who produced the articles on show, and the awarding of prizes to the workmen, rather than giving credit to the firms who employed them.

And he carried this concern for the interests of the worker to the point where an Act was passed providing protection for inventions—a much needed Patent Law reform which reduced the heavy fees payable by inventors.

Thomas Paterson was fully aware of the disparity between the status of men and women.

Emma summed up the support he gave her, in her preface to his book. "Not only did he afford me invaluable advice and aid in the formation of the Women's Protective and Provident League in 1874, and in its subsequent work," she wrote, "but he also most generously sanctioned the absorption of much of my own time in the movement."

5

People and Places

As a bookbinder herself—or at least a former apprentice bookbinder—Emma first made an approach to workers in this trade. But there were other considerations which made bookbinding a hopeful field to work in.

The London committee of the League had examined the results of Emma's first plan—to form a National Union of Working Women.

A union of this name was founded in Bristol, probably in September 1874. It thrived in the area and it was certainly still in existence in Bristol twelve years later. It included women in various trades and the idea was to be revived in later years when Mary Macarthur led the League. But in those early days, in spite of the union's local success, the central committee decided that separate societies for different trades were more practicable, certainly in London.

It is interesting that this National Union was accepted by the Trades Union Congress, whereas the League had to wait until resistance against the idea of admitting an association of "middle class ladies" had been broken down. Since the origins of the union and the League were pretty much the same, there seems to be something in a name.

Among bookbinders there was still anger among the women at the treatment they received during the great depression in this trade three years before.

Emma found an ally in Henry King, of the London

Consolidated Society of Journeymen Bookbinders. King had been secretary of his union for three years and was to lead it for another twenty-five. He had scored an early success by getting the agreement of employers to a nine-hour day. He died in 1903 at the age of seventy-seven after enjoying in retirement a union pension of 30s. a week for only four years.

King's union was a man's union and as things stood he could not open it to the admission of women. But he at once gave support to the forming of a union for women.

King offered the premises of his society for a preliminary meeting which was held on August 31. Twelve women came to that meeting. They agreed to spread the news among their colleagues in various parts of the trade and persuade them to listen to Emma at a mass meeting to be held almost at once.

As soon as the doors of Harp Alley schoolroom in Farringdon Street in the City opened on September 12, it was clear that it was going to be a good meeting.

One can picture the groups of women, young and old, some talking excitedly, some silent, keeping close together in awe at their own boldness, taking their seats in the schoolroom, chilled by the autumn air.

When Emma Paterson rose, she quietly acknowledged the applause, at first hesitant, then mounting almost to a cheer, from the 300 women in front of her. There were folders, sewers, gatherers, and in fact workers from all sections of the bookbinding trade.

It must have been a moment of fulfilment for Emma. But she did not allow herself to be self-congratulatory. She was well aware that this was a beginning only and that the real struggle was to come. Much now depended on her method of approach, and, as always with Emma Paterson, it was direct and uncompromising.

She related something of the unhappy experiences of the past and dwelt on the miseries of their present conditions. The women must take matters into their own hands. They could expect no willing reform among the employers and she made no bones about the need to manage their own affairs rather than rely on their fellow male trade unionists. They must at once form a women's society.

The women agreed overwhelmingly and with enthusiasm. They elected a provisional committee which was instructed to draw up rules and organise another big meeting in the following month.

At this follow-up meeting the rules were adopted, a committee of nine was formally elected and the first women's society was established with 300 members. Emma was made provisional honorary secretary but as soon as she was able to find someone to take her place she handed over the office.

Her successor, in the following year, was Miss Eleanor Whyte, a working bookbinder who kept the secretaryship until a few months before her death in 1913. After Miss Whyte's departure the society, by this time widely regarded as little more than a friendly society, also died.

It was always Emma's intention to give her societies early help but no unnecessary nursing. She encouraged the women to conduct their own affairs and elect their own leaders, always recognising that members could afford little in the way of cash contributions and would need financial help.

Soon she was able to leave the bookbinders to get on with their business and their recruitment, and turn her attention elsewhere.

A number of dressmakers had watched the progress of the bookbinders and now asked if they too could form a society.

The League offered them help if they would publicise a meeting. This took place in January 1875 when 400 women, dressmakers, milliners and mantlemakers, came to the Co-operative Institute Hall, Castle Street East, W. They formed a society and this was followed two months later by women employed in the binding, sewing and trimming of men's hats, a trade confined to south London.

They held a meeting in the Howe Congregational Church, Bermondsey, with the blessing of the Rev. J. Sinclair, and a third society came into being.

The upholstery women were next, and fifth came the shirt and collar makers after holding a preliminary meeting in the schoolroom of St. Martin's in the Strand.

From the beginning of the League until Emma had to leave active work through the illness which soon ended in her death, she found premises for its headquarters in the Holborn or adjacent Bloomsbury area. One could have said the League first saw the light of day in Castle Street, Holborn, except that this early home was a basement room into which little light of day penetrated.

Soon Emma was able to get better accommodation at Little Queen Street where there were two rooms on the ground floor at £40 rent a year. Even this was half the first-year's income of the League. At once she planned a reading and rest room where women could sit after an exhausting search for jobs, or consult registers of employment on offer. It was Emma's answer to the men's "house of call"—usually the local pub. Emma's house of call would be a quiet room for relaxation and reading. She at once began to build up a collection of books to form a library.

Castle Street ran into Drury Lane from the west while Little Queen Street met Great Queen Street at right angles at its eastern end. In 1905 Little Queen Street became part of Kingsway, the hundred-foot-wide artery divided by entrances to the former underground tramway to the Thames Embankment.

Great Queen Street was cut short by the building of Kingsway but on the other side of Kingsway a short remnant of the former Great Queen Street survives as Remnant Street.

It was from 31 Little Queen Street that the first issue of the Women's Union Journal was published in February 1876, and it continued there for two years when a demand from the landlord for more rent and a need to seek roomier premises decided Emma to change. The landlord was either William Mansell, shown as the "occupier" of the premises, or the Rev. John Parr, "owner".

She found what she wanted at 36 Great Queen Street. The landlord here insisted on letting more accommodation than the League could afford but by sub-letting they were able to keep the rent down to their £40 a year limit.

Emma reported to the annual meeting that "the rooms are more lofty, better ventilated and much larger than previously". Monthly social meetings, cramped before, could be held here in more comfort.

She found this new home for the League at Christmas 1878 but the tenancy of No. 31 ran until March of the next year, so the League had to pay double rent for a quarter.

They occupied the first floor at No. 36, showing a further move upward from the basement days of 1874 and the ground floor period at No. 31.

At the time of the move, 36 Great Queen Street was occupied by the British Medical Association. At present the building is owned by the Freemasons, who have their massive United Grand Lodge of England opposite. No. 36 has the Medical Eye Centre on the ground and Messrs. Allweather Evade Paints Ltd. above.

Great Queen Street was named after a Stuart queen. It

was built on part of the route taken by James I on his way to Theobalds, his favourite residence in Herts, and was the last (or first) built-up street on this side of London.

Emma and the League spent the next seven productive years, until the last year of her life, at 36 Great Queen Street. Then, once more a landlord's condition forced a move. A new landlord bought the premises and insisted that the whole house should be taken by one tenant. The League moved to the Industrial Hall at la Clark's Buildings, Broad Street, Bloomsbury. The new League headquarters consisted of one large room with a small office attached. It saved £10 a year on the rent, for here they had to pay only £30 a year.

The League later made another interesting move which linked it with the earliest period of Emma Paterson's working life. This will come later in the story.

EMMA PATERSON

6

Work in the Provinces

Activities were by no means confined to London. Bristol was the earliest scene of organisation. After reading her paper to the Social Science Congress at Bristol in September 1874, Emma addressed a conference in Bristol from which was formed the National Union of Working Women.

Unions for women were formed in Dewsbury and Leicester.

In Dewsbury women struck against a proposed reduction in wages. There was a lock-out which lasted six weeks and would probably have gone on longer. But the women workers, without a union when the dispute began, came together in an association under the League and the employers thought it expedient to make concessions.

A compromise settlement resulted and the women went back to work. In Leicester the hosiery workers had a champion in Mrs. Mason who, in 1877, was to go as a delegate to the TUC.

In Yorkshire, the determined Mrs. Ellis—who also became a TUC delegate—organised an eight-weeks' strike of weavers and then led the women triumphantly back to work.

Meetings were held in 1875 in Glasgow, Sheffield and Manchester.

Edith Simcox and Emma took charge of meetings in Glasgow which resulted in the formation of the Society of Glasgow Tailoresses; and in Sheffield women in the silver polishing trade were brought together but did not form a society. Emma called a second meeting and tried hard to get a union going but she had to report to the second annual meeting of the League held on June 29, 1876, that "there was no immediate result".

Emilia Pattison (later Lady Dilke) was a great help to the League in Oxford where a powerful start was made with the formation of a society in 1881. Mrs. Pattison invited local working women and interested friends to a meeting in her dining room at the rector's house at Lincoln College. It must have been a big dining room for it held 120 people and she gave them all tea.

Mrs. Pattison presided at this meeting and Emma Paterson spoke to good effect, for a strong society resulted. That the social side was not forgotten is shown by Mrs. Pattison's gift of a piano to the society.

But by and large the first year's work was concentrated on London, and the "explosion", as it would now be called, into the provinces did not begin until the latter half of the League's second year.

During the following years a pattern of small unions emerged, covering women dressmakers, upholsterers, bookbinders, artificial flower makers, feather dressers, lace, paper box and bag makers, tobacco workers, jam and pickle makers, small metal-workers, rag-pickers, shop assistants and typists. Soon sixteen unions for women were formed in the League.

They were all in comparatively simple trades. Emma and her helpers were realists enough to know too well that in the heavier industries the entrenched interests of men trade unionists would give them no hope of success with the organisation of women.

As it was, inexperience, the fragmentation of limited resources both in funds and womenpower, and the fear and apathy among the women themselves, made the task of union building as formidable as making houses with sand.

Many of the associations needed propping up and some had to be rescued from threatened disaster.

Emma was both architect and fire-brigade, and the astonishing thing is that she was able to keep up the central strength of her organisation while so many of its parts wilted or failed.

Her great sustaining power was her faith in the need for her work. Women must be shown what they could do— what, indeed, they must do.

And, she argued, they could have no lasting faith in their growing conviction of equality with men unless they took their place in that bastion of male working-class independence, the Trades Union Congress.

There is no doubt that one of the main obstacles to women joining trade unions has been the attitude and often open hostility of men in trade unions. This cannot be dismissed as sheer bloody-mindedness, however, and it should not be thought that this exclusion was in any sense an objective of male trade unionists.

Indeed, without the help of organised workingmen, Emma would have made little or no progress. Many unions held out a helping hand to women, welcoming them into their own ranks or offering to form women's sections— the Amalgamated Clothing Operatives, the London Compositors, the Printers, Warehousemen and Cutters, the London Cigar Makers, the Steel Smelters, the Tin and Steel Millmen, the Chain Workers, the Sheffield Hand File Cutters.

These and other unions were able to overcome prejudices among the large body of male workers, born out of the bitter struggle they had waged for so long against employers, many little better and some worse than slave-drivers.

Trade union organisation was not by any means entirely

a male fight, but it was, by the very nature of things, primarily so and rights won by blood, mental torture and every sort of human privation were jealously to be guarded.

When Emma Paterson came on the scene, it was less than half a century since the Combination Laws had been repealed, in 1824. Before that, any discussion about pay or conditions was illegal and went on only in secret. At the end of the eighteenth century there were more than forty Acts of Parliament to prevent workmen from combining.

As late as July 1800 a Bill was rushed through Parliament which confirmed that a workman "entering into a combination for obtaining higher wages, reducing hours of labour, or decreasing the quantity of work" could get three months in jail or two months with hard labour.

And if he tried to get other workmen to join him he would be liable to the same punishment. If, for instance, an uncle were to give friendly advice to a nephew that he should not work for "that old scoundrel so-and-so" he could go to jail.

And, of course, any meeting to discuss wages and conditions was illegal. It was even against the Act of 1800 to help strikers by collecting funds, and this measure was made retrospective, any money already collected for the support or maintenance of strikers being liable to confiscation.

As A. L. Morton points out in *A People's History of England*—in the heyday of *laissez-faire* two exceptions were made to the concept that State interference with industry was an infringement of natural law. One was when workers were legally forbidden to form combinations to improve their wages and the other when the landlords were able to secure the prohibition of the import of wheat.

Emma Paterson's work began in a trade union world in which some could still personally have known the Tolpuddle Martyrs or had an elder relative in the Peterloo massacre.

Men were having a hard time trying to get even a meagre
share of the growing prosperity of the country and a measure
of security with it. Many saw women not as their allies, but
as a threat to their efforts.

They feared employers would exploit women in order to
weaken their own organisation, and of course they were
right.

There was still much of the fear that inspired the potters'
union in 1845 to appeal to women working on the new
flat-press machine:

"To maidens, wives and mothers, we say that machinery
is your deadliest enemy. Of all the sufferers by mechanical
improvements you will be the worst.

"It is a systemised process of slow murder for you. It
will destroy your natural claim to homes and domestic
duties and will immure you and your toiling little ones
in overheated and dirty shops, there to weep and toil
and pine and die."

If women, with a reputation for undercutting rates and
diluting the labour force, were now to be organised, would
they not undermine the progress made towards improving
life for workers and their families?

Emma was impatient of this attitude and indeed went
beyond many of her contemporaries, male and female, in
advocating equality of hours and conditions for women as
well as wages.

But in tackling suspicious male attitudes she had the
disadvantage of having around her an array of middle-
class men and women who, however sincere, did not carry
conviction with every working man.

Emma wrote to the Trades Union Congress claiming that
the National Union of Working Women, with 300 members,
should be represented at the TUC. The union had affiliated

to the TUC but there was some hostility to the idea of representation for a gathering of "middle-class ladies".

Eventually Emma decided to send a man, H. M. Hunt, to the TUC. His address was given as 4 Queen Square, Bristol, where the NUWW was founded.

Objection was raised at the TUC to women being represented, but too much should not be made of this for it is certain that the general atmosphere was one of subdued acceptance.

It is worth quoting the single serious protest and showing how it was disposed of.

The Standing Orders Committee reported to the Trades Union Congress in January 1875, at the Concert Hall, Lord Nelson Street, Liverpool, that they had doubts about only two applications for representation at Congress.

One was from the Carpenters and Joiners in London who had failed to give details of their membership; the other "doubtful" was the National Union of Working Women.

This gave F. J. Whetstone, representing 44,000 members of the Amalgamated Society of Engineers, the opportunity for a speech in which he pointed out that this was the first time in the history of Congress (one would have thought the TUC was fifty years old; in fact it had been going only seven years) that they had had a representative of the female sex.

He gave women due credit for establishing their own trade unions but didn't think they should accept representation of their sex at Congress.

He drew a harrowing picture of the future possibility of a man sitting on one side of Congress representing one society and his wife on the other representing another society.

He thought women should not only have their own trade unions but also their own trades councils and their own Congresses.

Mr. Whetstone moved that Congress could not admit a representative from any female trade union.

The TUC chairman, James Fitzpatrick, then announced that the Standing Orders Committee had accepted credentials from the women's society, and that would be final.

His announcement gave general satisfaction to delegates. Mr. Hunt stayed and later in the week he spoke on the Workshops Regulation Bill which, he contended, was not wanted because the regulation of the hours of work for women and children would not be of benefit to those members of the community so much as of value to men.

There were cries of "No, no", as he went on to explain— and we cannot exclude his having been carefully briefed by Emma Paterson, who held strong views on this matter— that if females had the right to work they should also have the right to dispose of their labour as they thought fit.

This was a matter on which Emma herself was soon to have the opportunity of speaking to a Trades Union Congress.

A further dread expressed by Mr. Whetstone, in his protest against women delegates, was that if Congress accepted a male delegate to represent women, they would be bound to accept at any future Congress any delegate the women might send—and this delegate might be a woman.

To which there was a resounding "Hear, hear" from delegates.

In fact this is exactly what happened—and was intended by Emma Paterson to happen—in the following year.

7

Books and Baths

Trade unions today are not mere recruiting and negotiating machines with no thought for private and family comforts and amenities.

They offer facilities for education, convalescence and even entertainment and leisure pursuits to their members.

Emma Paterson saw, in those early days, that whatever the urgency to secure bread, women did not live by bread alone.

The payment of benefit began almost at once, and a meeting and rest place was opened at 31 Little Queen Street.

A register of available work saved members the crippling pursuit of jobs on foot. Newspapers which advertised work, such as the *Daily Chronicle* and the *Daily Telegraph*, were on view. It was from the *Telegraph* that Emma, in a speech, quoted a situations vacant advertisement: "A gentleman to travel in skirts and costumes", and made the comment: "After the first shock one discovers that the gentleman would be required to sell skirts and costumes, not to wear them." And, as might be expected, she added: "Why should not ladies become commercial travellers in skirts and costumes—and other articles of women's wearing apparel?"

Even when women—or men for that matter—got work they were not paid at once. Emma saw the need for loans in advance of wages. She arranged for these and later opened a bank, the Women's Halfpenny Bank, for those who found work and wanted to save against the day when they might lose it.

The bank soon had 200 depositors and members were taking a share in the management.

An early service was the opening of a library. Members paid sixpence a quarter and it was open to non-members at threepence a month and a deposit of a shilling unless they could supply an acceptable reference.

Here many working women for the first time found a world beyond the confines of drudgery. They could read travel books, biographies, history and other works. But there were fiction and popular magazines too.

There was nothing stuffy about No. 31—or any of the later premises where the League had its offices. Social meetings were held with music and singing, and the individual unions were encouraged to organise outings.

Emma's *Women's Union Journal* has frequent references to "excursions"—by the Society of Upholsterers to Epping Forest where 200 had tea at the Robin Hood Hotel and then walked in the forest and danced; or the Society of Women Employed in Bookbinding who took a train to Shirley Hills near Croydon.

A more sinister sound was the warning to workpeople of the injustices and frauds that employers practised on their "hands": Emma was early in the field with a department which every large union now has—a legal department. She announced that she would lay before the League's committee any cases that came to her notice with the object of obtaining redress.

A married mantle worker named Jessop earned 4*s.* a week and, driven no doubt to desperation by poverty, she took six jackets home. She was sent to prison for six weeks and Emma at once opened her own inquiry and proposed to her committee that the woman should have help when she left prison.

When members of the League took ill they were not left to suffer alone; visits were paid to the sick in an organised way.

The League was able, with funds provided by sympathisers, including Lady Goldsmid, to rent furnished houses in Margate and Brighton and offer members cheap summer holidays. Seaside holidays were in those days luxuries enjoyed by the well-off. Many working people went through their lives without so much as a glimpse of the sea.

The Brighton house, ten minutes from the sea with the Downs above, offered a room for three or four shillings a week in August and September with the use of a sitting-room and attendance. A notice to this effect told members that they could buy a third-class return ticket from London Bridge or Victoria on the London, Brighton and South Coast line for 7s. 6d.

These holidays were made possible by the help of wealthy friends, but Emma was reluctant to ask outsiders for money for League activities (Lady Goldsmid was a member of the League council).

Emma wrote in her *Journal*:

"We have no wish that the League should be included among the numberless societies which at the present season advertise, circularise and beg in every possible form. It is true the League is obliged to receive money help, although its main object is to assist in organising self-supporting societies of working women. But the committees seldom ask for money."

In 1886 it was recorded that nineteen visitors took accommodation, members of the League paying 3s.–4s. a week and non-members 5s.–6s.

Certainly Emma was never at a loss for ideas. She was critical of the strange clothes which convention imposed on women. It would have been interesting to see how women's fashions might have changed if the League had gone ahead with her proposal to design for women a "reformed rational national" dress.

She probably had in mind at one time opening a hotel for working women, for she gave much publicity to a project of this kind in the United States, and she was angry when it came to a sudden end.

The hotel appears not to have lasted long in its original guise. It was pronounced a failure, Judge Hilton, the executor of the original founder, asserting that working women would not use the hotel because they could not have the society of men there.

Emma indignantly denied that this was the real reason for discontinuing the original purpose and making it into an ordinary hotel. She declared that the real reason for failure was "difficulties" placed in the way of working women in the form of high charges and the enforcement of rules against domestic pets and sewing machines.

A proposal of Emma's, taken up with enthusiasm, had behind it a more serious motive than at first appears. This was a swimming club with lessons for women.

The Women's Union Swimming Club was formed in November 1878 and the League made arrangements with the St. Pancras Baths authorities for its members to use the "large tepid" baths in Whitfield Street, at the Warren Street end of Tottenham Court Road, each Wednesday from 2 p.m. to 10 p.m. at a charge of 2*d*.

The venture was an immediate success. By the third Wednesday it was attracting 214 women.

The formation of this club and its popularity was undoubtedly due to the tragedy of the *Princess Alice*.

E

River trips were a favourite outing for working people at the time. On the evening of September 3, 1878, an iron saloon steamer, the *Princess Alice*, returned from a trip to Sheerness with 900 people, mostly working women and children, came into collision in Gallion's reach, a mile below Woolwich Arsenal, with the steamer *Bywell Castle*. More than 600 passengers drowned in the Thames or died of their injuries.

This tragedy gave rise to a strong call to Londoners to learn swimming.

Emma Paterson was early off the mark with her club—and it was no short-lived craze either. Eight years later the club was flourishing—still at 2*d.* a visit on Wednesday evenings.

There was then, as a notice in the *Women's Union Journal* of May 1886 shows, a professional teacher, Mrs. Hawkins, offering lessons at 3*s.* a course with a prize competition at the end of the season as an added encouragement.

Meanwhile the mainstream of activity of the League flowed on with twenty-three public meetings in the first full year at which societies were either formed or strengthened and the objects of the League made more widely known.

Emma was not an out-and-out rebel, nor was she in the least desirous of producing rebels.

She declared the League to be conscious of the fact that many employers were friendly to her movement "from their own knowledge of the need for some provident organisation among their workpeople".

And, as she shrewdly pointed out, the League should find sympathisers (or even secret allies) among those employers who had a pride in their own "respectable" trading and suffered from the "unfair competition" of the sweating activities of those who practised the "slop" system of trading.

The *Women's Union Journal*, founded by Emma in 1876, introduced a feature giving the names of employers who paid fair prices to their workpeople—the names were supplied by the women themselves.

The object of the League, it said, was "to promote an *entente cordiale* between labourer, employer and consumers".

In the first report of the League its objects included the proviso that "a revision of the contract between the labourer and employer is only recommended in those cases in which its terms appear unreasonable and unjust to the dispassionate third party who pays the final price for the manufactured goods and is certainly not interested in adding artificially to their cost".

For all the work that went on during this first year, the accounts show a modest budget whose chief items were the hire of halls and advertising £20 2*s.* 1*d.*; printing etc. £28 13*s.* 9*d.*: and the rent of offices, cleaning, coal, gas and wood, £5 15*s.* 11*d.*

And in those days before London Transport, a year's omnibus fares (for how many people?) are shown in the accounts as a grand total of 4*s.* 4*d.* which would now be absorbed by a single twenty-minute journey on the Underground.

The League during this time became well known but not particularly feared by the employers who were too securely entrenched to be worried by a few hundred women banded together in law-respecting "societies".

The League gained strength through steadily growing membership and additions to the industries in which it was possible to found unions.

Emma herself was becoming a nationally respected leader of working women, trusted by men and women alike. It is significant that whatever fears were expressed when a man represented women at the Trades Union Congress in Liverpool in January 1875, no word of protest was heard when Emma Paterson, then twenty-seven, took her place at the eighth TUC in Glasgow on October 11, 1875, with Edith Simcox of Bristol.

They were the first two women delegates to attend the TUC.

And at once there flared up in the hall a controversy which parted Emma from some of her fellow campaigners.

She and Edith Simcox, with their natural honesty, made no attempt to put up a common front on this issue. They enlivened the debate with contradictory contributions which certainly owed nothing to factional discussion before the public proceedings, on the question of selective legislation for women.

8

First Call for Equal Pay

At the TUC Emma Paterson represented 275 members of the Society of Women Bookbinders and 92 members of the Society of Women Upholsterers.

Edith Simcox was delegate for thirty-nine members of the Society of Women Shirt and Collar Makers. H. M. Hunt of Bristol also attended as before, representing (it was claimed) 3,300 members of the National Union of Women Workers.

The TUC's first two women were received by other delegates without fuss or open signs of disfavour.

They told delegates something of the desires and aims of women in industry in a way that was fresh to that gathering, and however opposed the men were to the women's views on such questions as workshop legislation, Emma was able at a later date to pay this tribute to her fellow workers: "All the speakers were at least so good as to argue the question instead of making silly puns or howling down the speaker, as gentlemen in another place sometimes did when the interests of women were discussed."

It was this Eighth Trades Union Congress in Glasgow—a hundred years ago—which heard for the first time the view put forward seriously that women should get equal pay with men. Edith Simcox read a paper in which she said: "Hitherto the rate of women's wages have ended where that of men began. I would have women refuse to do men's work for less than men's wages." She believed women would unanimously agree with this if they could be made aware of the consequences which resulted from their working at the existing rate of pay.

When she spoke later on the question uppermost in the minds of people at the time—the regulation of hours of work—she said women would not object to a reduction in hours if it were not accompanied by a corresponding reduction in wages.

To this latter point Emma retorted that she would rather women suffer the evils of overwork so that they should in this way come more fully to an understanding of the unsatisfactory state of their position and of the need to form trade unions for themselves.

Legislation which restricted women's hours of work, she said, would give women the idea that they were sufficiently protected without combination.

Her attitude caused many delegates to draw breath and look sharply at this uncompromising woman.

Among them was Henry Broadhurst, the stonemason's secretary and a formidable member of the TUC's Parliamentary committee, who finished his political career as an Under-Secretary in Gladstone's Liberal government in 1886.

Broadhurst said they were glad to see unions formed by women but could not agree with Mrs. Paterson on the question of the extension of the Factory Acts to women. His union (the Operative Stonemasons' Society) had always devoted their efforts to the reduction of hours, which had always led to improved conditions and the increase in wages.

"To shorten the hours has ever been found the best way to improve the conditions of both men and women," he said—and Emma interjected "By union." Broadhurst: "Certainly by union if possible, but if not possible by union, then by some other means."

Then, to emphasise his disapproval of the stand taken by

this persistent woman, he went on to say that he thought the proper place for married women was in the home and that the effect of the improvement which had taken place in the condition of workingmen had been to withdraw from the labour market the competition of married women. This, of itself, had had great effect in raising the wages of women.

What Emma Paterson made of this argument can be imagined. It must have left her with a sense of despair of ever being able to educate trade union man into an understanding of trade union woman.

Emma herself was fighting a now-established tradition that selective law should give some protection to children and women. This began with legislation on hours of work in 1802 when meagre protection was given to very young children, and in 1819 the Cotton Factories Regulation Act forbade the employment of children under nine in cotton factories while those between nine and sixteen could work no longer than $13\frac{1}{2}$ hours.

The weakness was that, since there was no one to see the Act enforced, it became little more than an empty gesture.

In 1833, after the Reform Act was passed, and under pressure mainly from north of England workers, a new Act prohibited children under nine from being employed except in silk factories.

Silk was exempted because the textile employers argued that serious foreign competition would otherwise ruin them. (Apparently children of eight and under were keeping the silk industry alive in England; if this were so it was certainly not reflected in their rates of pay.)

With the 1833 Act factory inspectors were appointed to see that the conditions were respected.

For all this show of humanitarian principles, nine years later a report uncovered the frightful conditions under which women and children worked in the mines. This was the 1842

71

Report of the Commission on the Employment of Women and Children in Mines and Collieries.

The disclosures were so harrowing that Lord Shaftesbury could see nothing worth saving from this hell below earth. His Mines and Collieries Act of 1842 simply forbade the employment of women and children in the mines.

One might well ask why ruling class conscience should have been so suddenly affected by the thought of women and children working underground. Women and children had been working down the mines for 500 years without any significant change in the conditions regulating their employment. They went down with their husbands and fathers, and as one generation was lopped off by age or illness, another took its place.

As early as 1322 the death is recorded of the daughter of a miner called William Culhaxc from "lc damp" in the "colepyt" at Morley, Derbyshire.

Why, then, this sudden concern 520 years after the death of Mistress Culhaxe of Morley, for the welfare of female miners?

The answer is not to be found in the compassion of the ruling class. The answer lies in economics.

The employers wanted women (and children) out of the mines where they were—often too literally—a dead loss. Cheap labour was needed in the rapidly growing industries, particularly in textiles. Women and children could be used, too, as a weapon against the strengthening demands of men, bonded into unions, for a share in the new prosperity.

Emma Paterson was well aware that the new concern of the ruling class for women and children was a matter of self-interest.

One of the consequences of the intolerable conditions for women in industry had been the increase in prostitution.

In 1841 there were 3,000 brothels in London alone and

veneral disease was rife. White slavery was common. Incidentally there was a pornography problem at the time too. A thriving trade was carried on in "dirty" books, and the cheaper newspapers built up their sales on sex. The Obscene Publications Act of 1857 had little effect.

The next move in selective legislation was the Ten Hours Act of 1847. With its amendments and extensions in 1850 and later it limited the hours of work of women and young persons. And by doing so it tended also to limit the working hours of men. For instance, when women textile workers went home at the end of their shortened day it became uneconomical to keep factories open for men only. So the men finished earlier too. In many factories the men used the shorter hours of women as a lever in their own struggle for shorter hours.

But, as Ray Strachey points out in *The Cause*, "there were great differences between the two forms of protection. The protection of women was imposed on them without their consent; it was entirely inflexible. . . . The other, the result of the men's own combination, was far more adaptable."

Male workers certainly did not ask for legal protection against long hours; women, unorganised and at the mercy of employers, were regarded as in need of the protection of the law.

This, contended Emma Paterson, simply underlined women's helplessness. The way to end women's impotence was by organisation not legislation.

And when a Home Office inquiry in 1873 recommended a reduction in women's hours from sixty to fifty-four and a Bill to this effect came before the House, the opposition of the "feminists" killed it.

In March 1875 a Royal Commission was set up to inquire into the operation of the Factory and Workshops Acts.

73

Members of Emma's League were invited to a meeting at the League's offices to discuss the Acts and later to this conference. The conference, on April 28, was attended by 130 women and was addressed by Sir George Young, secretary of the Commission.

Emma later put her views, and those of her members, before the Royal Commission.

She now learned beyond doubt that she was not carrying many with her in her stand against protective legislation—and the law was certainly not altered by the Commission's report. Emma henceforth muted, though she did not abandon, her attitude to women's hours and the law. She was on firmer ground in her demand for women factory inspectors, a cause which she vigorously pursued to the end of her days.

At the Trades Union Congress Emma contended that men inspectors went round the workshops with the employers. Workpeople, men and women, were given no real freedom to speak. Edith Simcox told delegates about a meeting in London at which half the seventy to eighty women present said they had never seen an inspector. Certainly none could think of any benefit they had received as a result of an inspector's visit.

Miss Simcox caused laughter with her story of a woman who said that while she had not actually seen an inspector, she *had* seen his hat. This inspector drank sherry with the master while his hat was sent to the hatters to be ironed and dressed.

In her campaign for the appointment of women factory inspectors, Emma rowed against a stream of opposition to women entering the professions.

Women at that time were not able to study for a degree. Even at the University of London, founded in 1826 as a "progressive" university, women were not allowed to take degrees until 1878—a year in which Emma at least succeeded

74

in getting the TUC to carry a resolution demanding that working women should be appointed as factory inspectors.

But a TUC resolution was as yet merely a gesture. In the same year, at the fourth annual meeting of the Women's Protective and Provident League, Emma had to express her regret and that of her committee "at the refusal of the Home Secretary to receive a deputation of representatives of the women's trade unions" to discuss the Factory and Workshops Acts Consolidation Bill.

The committee had hoped to put forward the view that several of the new inspectors, whose appointment was provided for in the Bill, should be women.

Emma questioned whether the system of inspection of factories and workshops as it was then carried out was of much value. "But," she told League members, "so long as the system is maintained, your committee are strongly of the opinion that women as well as men should be employed as inspectors."

The need, not only for Emma's persistence but also for her vigilance, was demonstrated at the following year's Trades Union Congress. The 1879 Congress again discussed a resolution on the appointment of working men as factory inspectors—without so much as a mention of women. Many delegates, in fact, regarded the inclusion of women in the resolution as what would now be known as counterproductive.

Emma was on her feet at once. She moved an amendment including women. It was carried.

This procedure became an annual routine. No doubt the TUC committee hoped to catch Emma out in the end and pass a resolution on factory inspectors, omitting women. But the more they left women out of the resolution, the more determined was Emma Paterson that they should go in. In the end she drew from an exasperated TUC president an explosive protest at "femine unreasonableness and obstinacy".

In 1881 Emma held a conference to press for the inclusion of women in the team of inspectors. But still Parliament resisted the demand with an off-handedness which amounted to contempt.

On March 5, 1886, the year of Emma's death, her *Journal* reported that Lord Enfield asked in the House of Lords "whether any future appointments of factory and workshop inspectors ... of H.M. government would consider selecting a certain number of women inspectors".

Lord Thurlow replied for the government in familiar vein that the question was of great interest and extreme difficulty. The subject had occupied the attention of the Home Depart-ment for several years and it was still under consideration (cries of "Hear, Hear"). Some noble lords now began to laugh in anticipation of Lord Thurlow's predictable con-clusion: "There is no intention to appoint women inspectors for factories and workshops."

Although Sir Charles Dilke, the husband of Emma's colleague, Lady Dilke, had used his influence and office in the House of Commons to press for women inspectors he had been able only to get women appointed as local govern-ment board inspectors. And it was not until 1893, seven years after Emma's death, that the first woman factory inspector took up her duties.

9

Into Print

Throughout her life Emma retained an interest in the print trade, a man's domain in which women had been accepted to a limited extent. Emma now thought this foothold could be made stronger.

A certain amount of heavy work, such as lifting formes of type, could well be left to men. Most of the other work in a print shop was not physically arduous. Even the custom of standing for long hours before a case of type could be changed with a little re-planning.

Before the Women's League moved in its early days to 31 Little Queen Street, Holborn, the premises were occupied by William Mansell, a bookbinder. It may have been coinci dence; but Emma, the former bookbinder apprentice, must have had acquaintances in the trade.

An early association with print was in 1872 when, in her Women's Suffrage days, Emma planned with Miss Emily Faithfull, the setting up of women's printing societies. Emily was one of the first women to join Emma's League, though she soon had to resign her place on the committee because of her heavy commitments.

Emily Faithfull was born in 1835, the daughter of a Surrey clergyman. She rebelled against vicarage life and left home to pursue an independent career of her own. With Emily in charge, women ran the successful Victoria Press which was able to undertake any kind of printing. It set up the *English Women's Journal* and other high-quality publications. Men were employed to move the heavy chases and the women were able to set type perfectly well while sitting on three-legged stools. It seems that the men just preferred to stand.

The origins of the Victoria Press went back to 1859 when a society for Promoting the Employment of Women was founded with the Earl of Shaftesbury as president.

Industry was in need of skilled women, however much short-sighted manufacturers and bodies representing industrialists howled their anger and scorn at the idea.

Print was thought to be one of the trades suitable for women. Queen Victoria showed an interest in the employment of women as compositors, and when W. Wilfred Head opened a printing works to train and employ women, he called it the Victoria Press.

Head had a four-storey building in Harp Alley, Farringdon Street, near Fleet Street, and here he printed news, books and jobbing work. His women were soon working on their own, although men also had a composing room on a higher floor, moved heavy chases, and continued work at night when the women left off.

The women printed a monthly, *The Australian and London Gazette*, which the Printers' Register declared to be "not excelled by any paper published in Britain".

The Victoria Press made progress and in a few years was able to speak of success in these terms: "The present condition of the Victoria Press is a proof that females can be economically and advantageously employed in the printing business." But Head and his women printers had to keep up a running fight with other master printers and he was finally stung into writing a small book to defend his employment of women.

He had, he said, found women's "quick and correct

composition makes it remunerative both to employer and employed" and declared printing to be "a healthy, intellectual and profitable employment for females".

Then he declared his main purpose in writing about his work. "Innovation of any kind," he wrote, "is invariably attended with opposition. . . . Few innovations could have been so obnoxious to a large and powerful class—the printers of the metropolis and few have experienced such persistent bitter and unscrupulous opposition."

The Victoria Press's proprietor was continously being represented in the master printers' press as a mischievous and pig-headed failure whose women produced poor work and had to be rescued by male printers.

But Head and Emily did not give way and, by maintaining a high standard of work and good management, they were able to get enough business to defy their detractors.

Records of women in the industry go back to the origins of the printing press. Nuns, it is said, worked as compositors at the Ripoli Monastery Press in Florence towards the end of the fifteenth century. A hundred years later Jenny Hirsch carried on a printer's business in Boston, U.S., and Mary Catherine Goddard printed the first issue of the Declaration of Independence.

Thomas Beddoes's book *Alexander's Expedition* was, in 1792, set up entirely by a woman compositor called Madely who did the job so well that Beddoes, in an advertisement, recommended women for this work. He wrote: "Their nimble and delicate fingers seemed well adapted for the craft of the compositor—and it will be granted that employment for females is amongst the greatest desiderata of society."

More recently women in the print trade have not found Welcome printed on the mat.

The Typographical Society's *Monthly Circular* for August

1865 reported that a Bacup newspaper office "was closed to members of the typographical union owing to the employment of female labour", and the following year there was trouble with an employer who wanted to offer work to women; however, it transpired that this employer could not find the right quality of applicant—or perhaps thought it expedient not to do so.

There is a reference to women in the half-yearly report of the executive of the Typographical Association in 1860. Members of the union were told not to work in certain printing houses because they employed women. But in the same year Bessie Rayner Parkes bluntly told women that they should enter that preserve of men in spite of the familiar arguments against admitting women into printing—long hours of standing and the heavy lifting.

In 1871, following strikes by male employees, an Edinburgh printer decided to employ women. The census of that year showed 741 women printers in England. In 1874 eighty women were working as printers in Edinburgh alone.

The women were paid considerably less than men and their employment led to strikes among the men.

As late as 1879 the London Society of Compositors forbade their members to finish work set up by women.

In the same year the *Standard* threw in a shaft full of bitterness:

"What women ask is not to be allowed to compete with men, which the more sensible among them know to be impossible, but to be allowed the chance of a small livelihood by doing the work of men a little cheaper than men do it. This is underselling of course, but it is difficult to see why, when all is said and done, men should object to be undersold by their own wives and daughters."

And in another publication:

"This work is much more remunerative and far less toil-
some and irritating than the occupation of the average
nursery governess and we anticipate . . . there will be a
large addition to the number of women compositors. The
reasons assigned against their employment in this capacity
seems to be the outcome of pedantry, prejudice and
jealousy."

This outburst (in Capital and Labour), it should be said,
was in support of an effort to get back to work men who had
struck against the employment of women in a print shop.

A familiar argument against admitting women to the
unions was that since women's wages were half men's or
less, the women would not be able to keep up their union
subscriptions.

Forty years later the attitude of one section of the unions
at least cannot be said to have changed much to judge by a
lecture at the St. Bride Institute, near Fleet Street, on the
trade union position in the industry in 1918 or 1919, given
by F. A. Davies, assistant secretary of the London Society
of Compositors. Mr. Davies said: "It may be a shocking
thing that in 13,000 members there are only twenty women.
Every man has a woman to support . . . and that is the whole
position in a nutshell." He then went on, somewhat in-
accurately, to say that in all bird, animal and human life
"the female is economically dependent on the male".

He thought those who advocated training women as
printers were intent on throwing "the system of seven years'
apprenticeship overboard", which oddly contradicted his
contention that "the great mass of women were not intended
to be either the physical or intellectual equals of men".

Encouraged by Emily Faithfull's success, Emma determined to add printing to her own skills. She learned the
trade and joined Emily at the Victoria Press.

By 1876 Emma felt competent enough to open her own press. She founded the Women's Printing Society and kept it going with a fair degree of success until her death.

Her first society, as we know, was the Society of Women Employed in Bookbinding—and the London Society of Bookbinders was one of the unions she represented as the first woman delegate to the Eighth Trades Union Congress in Glasgow in October 1875.

The Society of Women Employed in Bookbinding quickly attracted nearly 300 members and after a year Emma was able to hand it over to a capable young woman in the trade, Eleanor Whyte. The society remained in existence until 1913.

In his book, *Women in the Printing Trades*, J. Ramsay MacDonald wrote that not until 1874 was there a determined and successful attempt to organise women bookbinders into a union. On September 12 of that year, he said the first society for women employed in bookbinding "was formed by Mrs. Emma Paterson, the pioneer of women's trade unions in England".

Ramsay MacDonald recorded that from the beginning the relations between the men's and women's societies (in bookbinding) were "most cordial".

Even before Emma's election to the TUC her women bookbinders were heard of in Congress. At the January 1875 TUC in Liverpool the chairman read Emma Paterson's letter in which she drew attention to the fact that among the London women bookbinders, who numbered 4–5,000, a trade union had been formed three months before and was steadily prospering. She pointed out that the women's union had been helped by a "men's union" in the same trade. Her unnamed friends were H. R. King and his London Bookbinders. King, secretary of the London Bookbinders, was one of the first trade union leaders to join the Women's Protective and Provident League.

Women bookbinders, as we know, had a long history of trouble—particularly with some religious societies, which in their fervour for the spread of Christian brotherhood sometimes forgot that this included sisterhood.

In 1825 the Society for Promoting Christian Knowledge reduced the price of its literature, forcing down the wages of bookbinders, and a few years later (1833) the wages of people producing publications for the British and Foreign Bible Society were cut again. The masters would have settled in the ensuing dispute but the Bible Society intervened with a grim-faced "No".

The men petitioned the Society with the plea that if the 200 women bookbinders, many of whose wages were 5s. 11d. a week—against a man's wage of over a guinea a week—had their money cut further, it would be difficult, and in some cases impossible, "for females to earn an honest subsistence by their labour", leaving the way open for "the seducers of female virtue".

The Bible Society was unmoved by this argument, and the dispute eventually died in confusion with a change in methods of pay and a cut in hours to ten a day.

Later, the society put all its bookbinding in the hands of a single firm, and by a stroke of irony this was run by a woman, Miss Watkins, a harder nut than the former male masters.

Miss Watkins's way of resolving the struggle between Christian charity and business principles was to cut women's pay back to an average of little over 5s. 6d. a week and increase the hours again to more than ten a day. It was claimed by the workers that as soon as a woman earned more than 7s. a week—and on piecework this meant real sweating: she had to bind a hundred pearl Bibles to earn 5s.—she was discharged.

On top of this, heavy fines were imposed on the smallest pretext.

A hundred women went on strike, led by the young Mary E. Zugg (who died, at thirty-three, of consumption and is buried in Bow Cemetery).

The men's union contributed £146 in this dispute to help their sisters, but the strike failed. Some women managed to get work elsewhere but others had to go back under the old conditions. Of Mary Zugg, little more than a girl when she led this major dispute, union secretary Dunning wrote: "Nothing could exceed the temper, moderation and firmness she displayed."

Ramsay MacDonald tells in *Women in the Printing Trades* of the rough and ready kind of organisation among women workers in the trade before they had a union. Certain workrooms would set their own standards. These would be jealously maintained even though another workroom in the same firm was satisfied with a less perfect way of work. Strict discipline was enforced, including wage regulation.

It is said that the women would inflict a beating on the odd one who failed to honour an agreement among themselves.

10

The League Overseas

Emma Paterson's work had an influence beyond the shores of Britain. A National Women's Trade Union League was formed in the United States—a happy closing of a circle, since the idea of starting women's trade unions in Britain took shape during Emma's honeymoon trip to America.

The National Women's Trade Union League of America was not formed until 1903, seventeen years after Emma's death, but its foundation curiously counterbalanced the origin of the British League.

Thirty years after Emma went to America and came back with ideas which crystallised into the forming of her League, an American economist, William English Walling, visited Britain and, impressed by Emma's League, returned home to launch the American League. No wonder Mary Macarthur, successor to the leadership of the British League, said during a visit to America (at the 1919 Convention of the National Women's Trade Union League of America, in Philadelphia), "I am not quite sure whether the Women's Trade Union League of England is your grandmother or your grand-daughter."

The idea was quicker in crossing the Channel than the Atlantic. In 1877 a party of League members visited France.

They returned with the news that attempts made in Paris to form a women's league had attracted police attention and official hostility.

Among the organisers was a sempstress, Mlle Raoult, who "became an object of suspicion to the authorities".

Police went to her meetings and spied on her in the hope of discovering "something treasonable or wicked in her conduct".

It was reported by the British League's members that some of those who had tried to form the League in Paris had suffered financially at work and some workingmen who attended a meeting had been fined on some pretext.

Emma and her League did what they could to help. They organised a fund to help pay the fines that the victims of the law in France could ill afford.

On December 3, 1877, *The Times* published a letter signed by Emma Paterson as honorary secretary of the Women's Protective and Provident League. It spoke of the "miserable pittance paid to women in various trades in Paris", and declared that French women had been in touch with the London society with the intention of organising a League on the same footing as the one established in London.

Since it had been impossible for the French organisers to get authority for public meetings, they decided to hold a private meeting.

Emma told in her quiet, terse way, what happened even before the meeting could take place.

"A police officer called upon the lady who was issuing the invitations for the meeting, asked to see one of the letters and after a little conversation requested the favour of a glass of water.

"The lady having left the room to fetch it, the officer at once searched for the rest of the invitations, found them and carried them off.

"These letters were printed forms with blanks left for the names of the persons invited; but the officer reported that they were being issued wholesale without any names. This was made the grounds of proceedings before the magistrate against the president, two vice-presidents and the secretary of the new society and a fine of £56 was imposed. If this fine is not paid within a few weeks, imprisonment will follow."

Emma pleaded for financial help for them.

But if the French authorities were touchy about rights of assembly, now recognised by the British ruling class, they were ahead in one respect which gave encouragement to Emma—they were ready to have women factory inspectors.

Emma reported in the *Women's Union Journal* of September 1878 that in the Department of the Seine, which included Paris, women were to be appointed as factory inspectors on an equal footing with men.

France had, at the time, only fifteen inspectors. It was now intended to appoint two chief inspectors and twelve inspectors. One of the chiefs and six of the rank and file were to be women.

Emma pointed out in her leading article that since in France only children and girls under twenty were covered by factory legislation and that in this country women of any age were covered, there was an even stronger case in Britain than in France for the appointment of women inspectors.

With this heartening news in her possession, Emma went to Bristol to take her place at the Eleventh TUC on Monday, September 9, where a motion on factory inspectors was to be put by Brother Birtwistle of Accrington. The motion called for "immediate action to secure the appointment of a number of respectable and practical working men as assistant inspectors".

Emma, even-tempered, frail-looking, tight-lipped, rose

with icy patience to her feet. She refrained from mentioning France. This was England 1878.

Would Mr. Birtwistle be willing to alter the wording of his resolution to include working women? Mr. Birtwistle considered. One is not told if he wore moustaches. If he did, one can almost see him stroking them with mock thoughtfulness as he agreed that he was willing to alter the wording of his resolution to include the phrase "and women where necessary".

This would no doubt have brought a rewarding titter from those delegates who were not disposed to admit working women to the exclusive ranks of factory inspectors to which even working men were not yet admitted.

Emma Paterson, still coolly diplomatic, said she did not think the words "where necessary" would meet the case. Delegates waited expectantly, like the audience at a game of chess. Mr. Birtwistle's move. He was now willing to substitute the words "practical workers" for "practical working men".

It seemed hardly necessary for Emma to point out that the words Mr. Birtwistle suggested would not be understood to mean women as well as men. Mr. Birtwistle no doubt showed surprise at this rejection of his final concession. He would go no further.

Emma Paterson proposed, and Edith Simcox seconded, an amendment adding "and women" after "practical working men".

It may be indicative of the attitude of Congress to these women and their strange demands that Emma herself, speaking to her amendment, admitted that she did not expect it to be passed. Or could it have been an indication of her skill at handling Congress? "But," she added, "if it is well supported it would be to good effect."

In fact the amendment was passed by 46 votes to 33. And

Emma, surprised, or merely satisfied that her impeccable manners had once more won the day, sat back no doubt to reflect that in the following year she would have to play the same part in a similar pantomime.

Three years later, in 1881, she certainly used the example of France at a conference she had organised to advocate the engagement of women factory inspectors. And at this conference she claimed that women could pass any examination which might be set to establish qualification for an inspectorship.

Places not requiring the passing of examinations should be divided, according to the terms she had piloted so skilfully through the Trades Union Congress, among "practical working men and women".

Among the many ways in which Emma brought women into the unions, the most dramatic was the organisation of the Royal Army Clothing workers in Pimlico, London.

Girls could, by working long hours at the depot and then taking work home to begin again at night, earn an admittedly good wage for those days. Some, it was said, made 30s. and more a week.

This, clearly, was a case for "reform" and the government arbitrarily reduced their rates, even for the majority whose pay came to nothing like the 30s. often quoted as normal.

Emma wrote in her *Journal* (May 1879) of the "ingenious" but "scarcely creditable" manner in which the government made the reductions.

On March 26, 1879, 1,500 women were discharged. They were told they could re-apply for their jobs within a "re-arranged" scale of payments. The practice became familiar later in industry and even today many council housing officers frighten their elderly tenants by giving them notice to quit when they want to put up the rents.

Frightened women besieged the depot but, no doubt as

an exercise in psychological warfare, the Army told them nothing.

Emma took a hall near the depot and organised a meeting. When this opened three weeks later, on April 16, 700 women tried to get in. Many had to wait outside, while news of what was said in the hall was relayed to them by word of mouth.

On the platform with Emma Paterson were Mr. and Mrs. Hodgson Pratt, the Rev. Stewart Headlam, Miss A. L. Browne and Emma's colleague at the TUC, Miss Edith Simcox.

The meeting was told about a whole range of cruel cuts. The rate for making an infantry tunic was reduced by fourpence to 3s. 2d. and an artillery tunic by sixpence to 4s. 6d.

It was agreed at the meeting that a deputation should go to the House of Commons preceded, "tomorrow", April 17, by a demonstration at the House.

Later, questions were asked in Parliament and Lord Eustace Cecil promised a committee to look into circumstances which were only too evident to government-employed women who had been brought down to the level of slop workers.

The Parliamentary inquiry, resulting from the massive protests led by Emma, was probably the first of its kind to investigate the grievance of working women at the demand of the workers themselves rather than on the advocacy of conscience-stricken upper-class or philanthropic bodies.

But the affair dragged on and reached no satisfactory conclusion. Continued vigilance and protest, however, almost certainly prevented further inroads into the incomes of the Army Clothing workers. The great positive result of this dispute was that Emma was able to organise women employed at the clothing depot into the union.

On Saturday, April 18, 1879, at the Westminster Democratic Club, the Westminister and Pimlico branch of the

London Tailoresses' Union was formed with an initial membership of 134 women employed in the Royal Army Clothing Depot. Emma Paterson was elected secretary. Soon the membership rose to 171. The women's solid achievement in terms of conditions was inconclusive but one more lesson had been learned—that even within the sacred precincts of a government establishment, women could organise themselves into a viable union.

11

The Journal

The *Women's Union Journal*, founded by Emma Paterson in 1876, was a remarkable publication. It was remarkable that it existed at all.

Trade unions at that time were about activity—protests, demonstrations and stoppages, as they often are indeed today, but mixed with the militancy was a certain piety, patriotism and awe of the ruling classes. This is shown even at a later stage in the banners of new unionist days where Utopia is depicted as a land where satisfied workers shake hands with benevolent bosses.

Certainly active unionists saw little need for the printed word other than leaflets, pamphlets and calls to meetings. They were not very good at regular publications to be taken home and read. They had neither the money nor the people to produce them and it is doubtful if many saw any value in them.

Some unions or groups of trade unionists produced journals, but few lasted long or made a noticeable impact.

The unions largely relied on more general publications like Lloyd James's *The Trade Unionist* or George Potter's *Beehive*, and on the fairness of some editors of the general press.

Emma had no doubt about the need for a publication for the League.

She had from the beginning shown a lively regard for the

THE *JOURNAL*

printed word—indeed she got the League off the ground with
printed addresses and articles.

And all her life she herself remained what newspapermen
today call "good copy"—a person they could rely on to say
something challenging or interesting.

In this sense of publicity Emma did not include self-
advertisement. She was passionately intent on getting her
ideas to the public, but it is a mark of her modesty that she
left little record of her personal life and personal thoughts
behind in print.

It has even been difficult to find a single picture of her.
Although there is mention of a picture of Emma in an office
at a later headquarters of the League it has not so far been
rediscovered.

The picture of Emma on the jacket of this book was re-
photographed from a copy of the *Illustrated Mail* of April 1,
1905. It accompanied an article about the League.

Emma started her *Journal* in February 1876 at the same
time as she opened the Women's Printing Society in Westminster. The Society printed the *Journal* which she edited
for the rest of her life. She wrote the leader and much of the
other material, including reports of the League's activities
and addresses delivered by its officers in various parts of the
country.

She led campaigns in its pages and was well aware of the
special impact made by large type and unusual treatment,
as when she increased the size of body type for a front
page report on the *Pall Mall Gazette*'s exposure of low pay
which, it was said, was forcing women on to the streets and
children into crime. She had large body type set across the
width of the page and the headline "The Pall Mall Gazette
Revelations" also in large type across the top of the page—
sensational treatment in those days.

She used the *Journal* for rallying calls, earnest declarations of faith: "A fair field and no favour is the treatment women most need in all the new paths upon which they are now entering."

Any editor will say that the letters his publication receives from its readers are a clear guide to the journal's success—and no letters are the most stinging comment of all.

Emma's *Journal* carried a great deal of lively correspondence, ranging from fashion comments to learned dissertations and thoughtful analysis of the League's policy.

Among the most moving tributes to the *Journal* were letters from two miners, published in the issue of December, 1880. William Crawford of the Durham Miners' Association wrote:

"Enclosed is eighteen stamps being twelve months' subscription for the *Women's Union Journal*. I am very pleased to see such a useful periodical devoted to the interests and social emancipation of women."

And Benjamin Pickard, writing from the Miners' Offices, Wakefield, said:

"I am struck forcibly with the idea that so far as being able to manage and support a trade journal the women are far ahead of the men. Many a time during the latter half of the nineteenth century have workmen essayed the issue of a trade journal, but I believe in every case they have failed miserably."

One of the earliest letters, in the second issue of the *Journal*, in March 1878, came from "Professor J. Ruskin, Corpus Christi College, Oxford", whom Emma had asked if he approved of the women's union movement.

"My dear Mme (wrote John Ruskin), I have entire sympathy with the motives which urge the present endeavours to enable women to obtain due wages—but they are complicated with the definite error of endeavouring to make the sexes independent.

"If you will look at 'Fors Clarigera' (Fortune, the club bearer. Ruskin used this as a title for a series of letters he wrote to British working men) you will find its constant principle is that the men of a country must maintain the women or they are worse than beasts.

Truly yours, J. Ruskin."

Many of the *Journal*'s readers sent poems and articles, and it published serials of personal experience.

Emma did not sign her own articles but there was never any doubt who wrote them. On one small item she allowed her identity, in the form of the signature "The Editor", to appear.

This was a simple, almost formal, account of the funeral of her beloved husband, Thomas. Other hands wrote the tributes, she permitted herself merely to record his interment.

Emma, who in later life regretted she had not found more time for her great joy in reading books, made time amid all her work to read widely in current affairs, overseas as well as in this country. The *Journal* is studded with items of interest, usually concerning women, from all over the world.

She would note a book in Italy set up by women printers, a hotel in America opened for women, the astonishing cloak-and-dagger reaction of the Paris police to an attempt to form a League-like organisation in France.

She publicised new services offered by the League and kept up to date with their progress—the swimming club, the libraries—the *Journal* often carried lists of books newly contributed by well-wishers—outings, socials, meetings, information about work available and holidays at favourable rates to members.

But one of the chief functions of the *Journal* was to hold together all the ends of the League that could otherwise have become loose and may at times have floated away out of sight.

She recorded the opening of new societies, published reports, often in detail, of the established ones, kept a record of meetings, including of course the League's internal meetings, and told her members what their officers were doing at the Trades Union Congress. She selected from the TUC those parts of the proceedings which helped her particular interests and those of the League.

In the pages of the *Journal* she kept up a persistent, if at times muted, campaign against selective legislation for women and an even more urgent agitation for the appointment of women factory inspectors.

Of the former, the controversy about women in nail and chain forges poured through the pages of the *Journal* in 1884, overflowing into her leader column.

A TUC resolution urging that an amendment to the Factories and Workshops' Act should bar girls under fourteen from factories forging nails, chains and bolts or other articles of the kind made from iron and steel, incensed women delegates, although Mrs. Wilkinson of the Upholsterers' Society seconded Mr. Juggins of Darleston's motion, with the comment that boys as well as girls needed protection.

The mover said that in South Staffordshire and East Worcestershire girls of seven, eight and nine were making nails and chains, which he regarded as a disgrace to the sex.

Mrs. Wilkinson's mild proviso did not spell out clearly enough the objection of other women delegates, and Mrs. Ellis of the Huddersfield Heavy Wollen Weavers' Association proposed an amendment to strike out the word "female" so that the resolution should apply to both sexes.

Emma Paterson seconded this amendment and, as she recorded in the *Journal* of October 1884, she made her position perfectly plain: the law was not, as far as she was concerned, to be the gallant knight riding to the rescue of maidens in distress. She saw through gaps in the shining armour and detected signs of a monster beneath.

Emma pointed out that only four or five years before there had been a great outcry against the employment of women in tailors' workshops—the indignation at that time was based on fears that the sexes working together led to immorality.

Emma scorned this reasoning, having in mind no doubt the unlikelihood of the sweated conditions of the trade providing opportunity for more than a tired smile passing between boy and girl.

She called such attacks baseless and sensational and pinpointed the real purpose behind them: they should, she said, be received with caution. "It was never proposed to turn men out of work by law—only women."

Henry Broadhurst, M.P., would have none of this feminine claptrap and even questioned the good faith of the women who put forward and seconded the amendment. He thought their purpose was to undermine the original resolution by ridicule.

However desirable it was to prevent boys of under fourteen working in this way, they knew perfectly well that it was utterly impossible that such a proposal could be carried. Mr. Broadhurst suggested the proposal was made "to elevate the female sex", as if that were the last thing anyone should want to do. But Emma's uncompromising insistence on equality of the sexes now led her into a self-made trap.

Broadhurst threw out a challenge. He urged Mrs. Ellis and Mrs. Paterson to visit blacksmiths' shops and see for themselves "the disgrace to this boasted civilisation of ours" in the degraded position in which women were to be found there.

His ringing challenge fell at Emma's feet like a wet sock. She had visited the shops, she said, and found the girls singing hymns. They looked strong and healthy.

Was she arguing for the employment of boys *and* girls in heavier types of industry, or against either being so employed? Mrs. Ellis must have winced.

The resolution was carried, the amendment fell, but Emma did not leave the question there. Her leader in the following month's *Journal* carried her own challenge. She proposed that Mr. Juggins, the mover of the resolution, should invite women to join his trade union rather than try to "ameliorate their condition by the harsh and undeviating operation of a law forbidding them to work". And with the touch of the professional, Emma followed her leader immediately with an amateurish working-class poem written by John Coley. It began:

> Mail masters are hard-hearted,
> They on the nailers frown;
> They always take delight
> To keep our wages down.

The poem takes us through some of the injustices in the industry and ends with an artless and authentic touch:

> My friends that stand around
> I hope they'll think this right,
> I made these lines my own self
> When it was dark at night.

On the question of women factory inspectors, it must have been with deep satisfaction that Emma extracted, for her *Journal*, from the proceedings of the 1885 Southport Trades Union Congress, her last Congress but one, the adoption,

without prompting, of two words which she had fought all
her days at the TUC to have included in its annual resolution
on factory inspectors.

Her report read:

"The resolution recommending the appointment of
practical working men *and women* as sub inspectors in
factories, so often a bone of contention at previous
Congresses, was unanimously carried and one delegate,
Mr. Drummond of Glasgow, who was formerly very
much opposed to the appointment of women as inspectors,
spoke strongly in its favour."

Emma did not, in her *Journal*, permit herself the jubilation
of italicising the two vital words "and women", but I have
done so on her behalf.

12

The End of Her Work

Emma had the full co-operation of her husband and relied on him for discussion and encouragement. She had another great friend in her mother who, following the death of Emma's beloved father, became her confidante as well as housekeeper, secretary and cook, "saving the unworldly couple", as the December 1886 *Women's Union Journal* said following Emma's death, "from the material inconveniences that arose from their common habit of paying more attention to meetings than meal-times".

Love, care and the settled background provided by Mrs. Smith for her daughter and son-in-law, enabled Emma in those early days of the League to be busier and happier than most women.

She was becoming a public figure, taking her place with equal ease at the tables of the great and in the parlours of the poor. She was a warm, if at times aloof, woman, and her dependence on a happy home background was greater because lack of time prevented her making intimate friend-ships outside the home.

She was unselfconscious about her own growing reputation as a political figure, although she was, perhaps, as her own *Journal* assessed after her death, "in some ways the ablest member of the first generation of English women who have entered seriously into political life".

While she found allies among the clergy, she had little

time for religion and was visibly startled when she first attended meetings of militant Scottish working girls in Glasgow. The girls were eager to build trade unionism but just as determined to maintain their custom of opening meetings— even trade union meetings—with a prayer.

Emma was certainly far from approving the current practice of mixing moral, charitable and religious sentimentality into the work of helping women to gain their rights. Her motivation was political and if the clergy were willing to help on this understanding, well and good.

On one occasion she risked the goodwill of her friends among the clergy by attacking the introduction of prayers and "virtuous" activities into women's clubs.

At a conference on women and industry called by religious interests at the Chapter House, St. Paul's Churchyard, in April 1879, she spoke of a woman's club "recently started by some clergymen" which had a rule that hymns and prayer should be provided at the closing of the club every evening.

Emma told the clergymen present that the practice would probably keep away the girls who most needed the influence of the club. And she added for good measure:

> "Wherever women go it seems to be thought the right thing to thrust needlework into their hands; no one has yet held a father's meeting at which work is carried on."

In spite of the doubts in her expressed by the suffragettes, Emma's ability as a leader—that is, a person whom others were proud to follow—is beyond question.

There is trust, respect and devotion in the tribute of one of her oldest and earliest League members: "I first saw her in September 1874. I shall never forget it. I was won from that afternoon and ever after did my best to do what she wished me to do."

101

She had the ability to judge quickly whether a person would be useful to her cause or otherwise. She would at once discuss plans with those she decided to trust and, after a few short, sharp questions, would put on a guarded manner with any she considered self-seeking, vain or idle.

With a large number of accomplishments, to which she was always adding, Emma refused—except to a limited extent in a later life—to allow her income-earning potential to deflect her from her main purpose in life.

She was a bookbinder and later a printer, a linguist, a teacher, an accountant and a shorthand writer with other secretarial qualifications. Her mastery of economics was impressive.

While she did not spare herself, and brought about her own early death through her refusal to slow down under failing health, she knew how to take leisure on the rare occasions when she and her husband were able to break away together.

There is a happy contrast between the story of her light-hearted complaint that the 3 a.m. collection of post near her home kept her writing letters between midnight—when she gave up other work—and that hour; and the account of her escape into the countryside with Thomas, when she would keep him walking for a blissful week or two at the rate of twenty miles a day.

They even spoke of plans to retire in their old age to a farm in the remote countryside, but neither came anywhere near old age—nor the state of modest affluence required.

When Thomas Paterson died on the night of October 14, 1882, at forty-seven, his failure to pay attention to the financial side of his life became evident in the debts he left. In a letter at the time about Thomas's burial, his sister Elizabeth declared that her brother had died "insolvent and intestate".

Even then Emma had no thought of using her talents to procure herself a comfortable living, as well she might. She merely cut down her expenditure. She excused notes on scraps of paper to a colleague by explaining that this was part of her "experiment" of trying to live on 6*d.* a day.

Emma was now alone, for her mother had died some years earlier. While she went about her work as before, the lustre had gone from her life.

She became ill—she was contracting diabetes as was discovered later—and at this late hour, after spending her own savings on one or other of the societies in which she was interested, she agreed to accept a small salary from the printing society for which she did regular proof-reading.

But her eyesight was failing and short spells at this close work was all she could manage.

However, poor eyesight did not keep her from meetings. She went to Portsmouth to look into a strike of stay workers, she spent days in Whitechapel organising girls in tailors' workshops into a union, she read papers at Oxford (a notable one at Balliol in February 1884) and spoke at a conference on industrial remuneration.

But in the summer of 1885, after the League's annual meeting, she became more seriously ill. Her friends found her "fevered and wasted" and she was persuaded to visit Dr. Elizabeth Garrett Anderson.

Elizabeth Garrett Anderson had herself known the struggles of a woman determined to overcome the crippling disadvantage of being a member of the wrong sex. She came of a suffragette family, and had decided, in 1859, to study medicine. But no British medical school would take her.

She went to the Middlesex Hospital as a nurse and "by all kinds of feminine dodges" persuaded the doctors to allow her into lectures and even into the dissecting-room. There was one possible examination which could give her a medical qualification. This was the Apothecaries. She passed the examination easily. Later, in 1869, she obtained an M.D. degree in Paris.

At the time only one other woman doctor was practising in England. This was Dr. Elizabeth Blackwell, who had qualified in America and in Paris, and whose example had inspired Elizabeth Garrett Anderson to study medicine.

Since foreign medical degrees were now excluded from the British Medical Register and, after Elizabeth Garrett Anderson's success, the Apothecaries' Society was barred from giving women degrees, it was a long time before she and Dr. Blackwell were followed by other officially accepted women doctors, although a few women, who qualified abroad, practised without licence in this country.

Dr. Garrett Anderson decided that Emma was a very sick woman and ordered her special diet, rest and travel to a milder climate.

So, at the beginning of 1886, while Edith Simcox took over the acting secretaryship of the League and edited the *Journal*, Emma went to the Channel Islands for a few weeks and returned apparently in better health. But soon the diabetes flared again. She had gone back to her work and, on November 29, after a visit to Tunbridge Wells, feverish though she was, she sat up late writing letters at her home, 23 Great College Street, Westminster.

On the following day, Tuesday, she was weaker and she found breathing difficult. But she demanded the proofs of the November *Journal* to correct. That night she became unconscious. With a cousin and sister-in-law at her bedside she died on the night of December 1.

Emma Ann Paterson was buried on Monday, December 6, at Paddington cemetery, Willesden, after a short service conducted by her friend, the Rev. Stewart D. Headlam, a member of the League's earliest committee. The wreath-covered coffin was lowered into the same grave as her husband in the presence of trade union leaders, secretaries of her own women's league unions and many friends and colleagues. Henry Broadhurst, M.P., represented the TUC.

13

What Happened to the Fund

At the thirteenth annual meeting of the Women's Protective
and Provident League on November 29, 1887, just a year
after Emma Paterson's death, it was reported that efforts
would be made to raise subscriptions for the establishment
of a central trades hall as a memorial to her.

It was hoped to get enough to form a working women's
club and institute and lodgings for single women. For this,
it was said, between £3,000 and £5,000 would be needed.
Among those who encouraged the idea was Florence
Nightingale, an old supporter of the League. Two years
later the Emma Paterson memorial fund stood at £513 and
a year after this it had risen to £870.

A proposal now came from the Working Men's Club and
Institute Union that funds which the club had raised should
be combined with the Women's League's fund to secure a
building for both organisations which would have separate
offices and club rooms for each society but with a central hall
which each could use.

The Women's League was reminded that Emma Paterson
was a former secretary of the club and that her husband had
devoted many years of his life to the club.

The Working Men's Club and Institute Union opened a
fund after Thomas Paterson's death in 1882. Seven years
later (1889) the trustees of this memorial fund handed the
balance of the fund to the Club. It amounted to £40. 7*s.* 7*d.*,

and was made up to £50 which, invested, amounted in 1912 to £100.

The Emma Paterson fund stood at £870 in 1890 and the following year at £1,085. In 1892 it had reached £1,700. The Working Men's Club and Institute Union was now having alterations made to a building at 2 Clerkenwell Road. A handsome frontage was being built with two separate entrances, one for the Club and the other for the Women's League. There were plans for roomy offices for both organisations.

In April 1893 the *Women's Trade Union Review* reported: "It is expected that the new offices of the League in Clerkenwell Road will be ready for occupation by the autumn."

In fact, in July of that year, the *Women's Trade Union Review* was distributed for the first time from the Clerkenwell Road address and it was also given as the offices of the League.

The Paterson memorial fund was still growing slowly towards the £2,000 to be paid to the Working Men's Club and Institute Union and now with £100 from Lady Goldsmid and a loan of £50 from Lady Dilke, the League discharged its undertaking and the deal with the Working Men's Club and Institute Union was complete.

The new Club Union building was officially opened on September 15, 1893 (although it had been occupied since the spring). A description of their new headquarters was published in the *Women's Trade Union Review* of October 1893:

"The Women's Trade Union League (as it had now become) has moved into its new offices at last, and very imposing they are.

"On one side of the building is the entrance of the Workmen's Club and Institute Union, while on the other is the entrance of our offices.

"Upstairs there is a small inner office of the League's secretary, Miss Holyoake, opening into a large outer office where the members of the London unions can meet, with the library arranged in bookcases against the wall, and two big Turkey carpets on the floor. . . . There is a great room in this building which can be procured for mass meetings. . . . Altogether the new offices are a great success and it was about time that a body which has affiliated unions all over the country and is connected with 45,000 organised women, should have central offices of proportionate importance."

In the League's annual report of 1893 reference appears to the "handsome offices and hall erected to the memory of Mrs. Emma Paterson, the League's founder". A Paterson Club for social meetings of League members was announced in the report.

Money was still required by the League to pay off professional charges, and to buy furniture and the fund remained open for this purpose.

14

Where the Members Went

"What will become of the League, how will it go on without her?"

This question was in most members' minds when Emma Paterson died. It was voiced and answered in the issue of the *Women's Union Journal* of January 1887, immediately after her death.

In a leader probably written by Lady Dilke (Emilia Pattison), credit for the greater part of the work accomplished by the Women's Protective and Provident League was given to the personal exertions of Emma. The writer went on: "But there are still upon the executive committee some who have worked with Mrs. Paterson from the first formation of the Society: many of the more recent members have been elected upon her suggestion and none without her concurrence."

This may not be a model prescription for the democratic running of a trade union organisation, but it must be remembered that trade unionism for women was still largely a benevolent exercise and the new unionism was not yet established.

The conclusion of the writer in the *Women's Union Journal* was that "the work of the League must go on".

Lady Dilke stepped into Emma Paterson's place for a short time. She was helped by Edith Simcox, and in 1887 Miss Clementine Black was appointed secretary. Lady Dilke was able to enlist the valuable parliamentary services of her husband, Sir Charles Dilke. He was an M.P. and a member of the Central Committee of the National Society for Women's Suffrage. He was always ready to use his influence in the interests of women's trade unionism.

In Emma Paterson's later years it had become clear that the building of massive national trade unions for women was a goal that would not be reached. Membership of any particular women's union—and Emma founded more than thirty during her twelve years as secretary of the League—remained small and even with constant attention they often wilted and died.

The total paid-up membership in the League at her death was less than 3,000, although the number of women trade unionists in the country was vastly greater (there were 30,000 in the cotton unions alone).

So the League changed its aims, advocating the acceptance and encouragement of women into membership of general trade unions.

Shortly before her death, Emma Paterson suggested that the name should be altered to the Women's Trade Union League.

In 1889 this advice was partly followed. The Women's Protective and Provident League became the Women's Trades Union Provident League and two years later this was shortened to Women's Trade Union League—Emma's preferred title.

Another change in direction was away from Emma's hard-line equality at all costs—indeed she had wavered on this issue herself in her later years—towards an acceptance that protection of women by law in their working conditions might not be a bad thing after all.

Lady Dilke now led the League into a campaign to get the hours of laundry workers cut from the eleven hours a day many were working.

This campaign was not immediately successful, but it did raise the pressure which four years later resulted in laundry workers' hours being limited to sixty a week.

The League also pressed for men's unions to take in women.

But it was in 1903 that the big change came in the running of the League—a change which may be said to have led it to its glorious extinction.

Lady Dilke was in poor health, her niece, Miss Gertrude Tuckwell, was honorary secretary and, with the resignation of the then full-time secretary, Mona Wilson, the League was in need of a dynamic person to take the general secretaryship.

Lady Dilke asked Margaret Bondfield, organiser for the National Amalgamated Union of Shop Assistants, to take the job. But she would not leave her shopworkers. However, Miss Bondfield had an idea, and this is the way Miss Tuckwell described the emergence of the most exciting personality to join the League since Emma Paterson: "The search for a successor looked hopeless when Miss Bondfield asked me to see a young Scotch girl, a member of the Shop Assistant's union. . . . She (Miss Bondfield) came to my little Westminster flat bringing a tall slip of a thing dressed in black, very silent, but intensely attentive, with that air of subdued excitement which made one feel the air alive all around her. . . ."

So Mary Macarthur, twenty-three-year-old daughter of a Tory shopowner, took office in the couple of rooms, without typewriter or telephone, that were the League's headquarters in the Club Union Buildings at the junction of Theobald's Road, Clerkenwell Road and Gray's Inn Road in London's densely built-up Holborn.

Mary Macarthur built the League into a great force of women, returning to the original idea with which Emma Paterson began.

Mary formed a National Federation of Women Workers, just as Emma had formed a National Union of Working

111

Women in Bristol in 1874. In two years Miss Macarthur had a membership of 2,000 in seventeen branches affiliated to the TUC. She shared her time and leadership between the two organisations—the League, and the Federation which drew in women membership from other unions.

In 1916 women's organisations, including the Women's Trade Union League and the National Federation of Women Workers, set up the Standing Joint Committee of Industrial Women's Organisations, with Mary Macarthur as chairman, to ensure that women were represented on government bodies.

In spite of her success in organising women, Mary was well aware of the forces working against the permanent segregation of one sex. Women joined the League and the Federation by the tens of thousands, but the turnover of membership was immense and the problem of holding women and persuading them to manage their own affairs was apparently insuperable.

She planned to absorb her women into general unions and organisations, and opened talks with the National Union of General Workers, later to become the National Union of General and Municipal Workers.

Many years before, Will Thorne's National Union of Gasworkers and General Labourers—an earlier name for the National Union of General Workers—and the new militant unionists, had shown a healthy interest in recruiting women into unions.

Now Mary Macarthur completed her negotiations with Will Thorne, still general secretary, and J. R. Clynes, president, of the NUGW, for her entry into the union at the head of 40,000 members of the National Federation on January 1, 1921. They were to form a separate women's section of the union. On the morning of that day Mary Macarthur died.

It had been agreed that Margaret Bondfield should accompany Mary Macarthur, as an officer, into the union.

Now it became Margaret's sad task to take Mary's place at the head of her members.

The new women's section of the union was classified as a district, but two years later the women members were integrated into the general membership with Margaret Bondfield as the union's first national chief woman officer. Later she entered Parliament and became the first woman Cabinet Minister.

The membership she took into the General and Municipal Workers' Union formed the nucleus of a massive women membership which now totals more than 270,000, more women members than in any other union.

Members of the Women's Trade Union League took a different direction. They became the women workers' group of the Trades Union Congress and two seats were allocated to women on the general council.

The women workers' group, with Margaret Bondfield as its chairman, came into existence in 1922 and in 1931 it became the national women's advisory committee of the TUC.

One further present-day institution in the trade union movement should be taken back to its origin with Emma Paterson. On September 20, 1877, she made an innovation at the TUC then being held in Leicester. She invited delegates to a meeting in the evening to consider the condition of women's work. It attracted more than seventy delegates, including the president of Congress, D. Merrick.

The idea was revived in 1926 and it was then proposed that the general council should present a medal for the best effort of any rank-and-file woman on behalf of the trade union movement. The custom of presenting a gold badge to a woman trade unionist at Congress remains an annual event.

H

15

Summing Up

What were Emma Paterson's achievements? When you count them on your fingers they seem so few: a group of trade unions founded—and often foundered; a League office serving a few hundred women and girls as an oasis of rest and dignity in a world of harassment and humility; a printing business entirely run by women; the introduction of women into a man-run Trades Union Congress.

Not bad, one supposes, for twelve years' work, but nothing so startlingly new.

Emma, I think, should be known as a great teacher. As a schoolteacher she would readily have admitted herself a failure. As a teacher of women in a belief in themselves, a sense of their right to equality rather than to a few privileges kindly bestowed upon them or even wrung from a man's world.

She organised, she wrote, she spoke to small groups and to masses, and she lectured at Oxford.

She was a frail, delicate person with a quiet austere countenance which seldom showed signs of passion. But the passion was there fuelling her controlled fire. She never tied herself to a railing—though this has its place in the scheme of things. She achieved her effects, her influence over people, with facts, tact and the force of argument backed by the conviction that women began equal, must always be equal, and should insist on sharing human rights equally with men.

Above all, she helped women in the factories and work-shop and in their homes, where the sweating continued at night, to find the time and the will to be women, to manage their own affairs, and to scorn concessions on ground of sex alone.

Emma collected around her the progressive intellectuals of her day, but she was never impressed or swamped by them. She drew out the best in her helpers and there was an astonishing sense of comradeship among these people of strong personality among whom conflict could have been expected.

They did not always agree with Emma, but her personal relationship with dissenters remained intact—so long as they worked as well as talked.

No one before her worked in this wide, unpromising field with such persistence and lasting effect. Her individual women's unions, mostly in the needle industries, mushroomed and sank, but her movement lives on, and working women have never been the same since.

Emma Paterson has been tucked away, forgotten and undervalued. She should be better known.

Appendix

This is the full text of an article by Emma Paterson published in Labour News, *April 1874. As a result of the appeal in this article a conference was called and the League formed.*

THE POSITION OF WORKING WOMEN, AND HOW TO IMPROVE IT

It is seldom disputed that the rate of wages paid to women is, in many occupations, disgracefully low. This may not be so glaringly the case in the great mills and factories of the North, but, in addition to cases which privately come to the knowledge of everyone, disclosures are not unfrequently made in the newspapers, showing how sadly many working women need some improvement in their position.

Not long ago a case appeared in the London papers which must have horrified all who read it. A woman had been working in a white-lead factory near London; the factory was three or four miles from her lodging; she had to walk to and fro morning and night. She could not pay the smallest amount for riding, nor provide herself with proper food, for her wages were but 9s. per week for work occupying twelve hours each day. She bravely battled with her difficulties for some time, and managed to keep alive herself and three children, but, at last, nature could hold out no longer; she died, and her death, leaving the children unprotected, brought to light the fearful tale. Had she supported herself only, the facts might never have been known.

Not only are women frequently paid half, or less than half, for doing work as well and as quickly as men. The following statement, made by a large manufacturer on the occasion of a recent deputation to the Home Secretary, shows that they are sometimes paid much lower wages for superior work: "Skilled women, whose labour required delicacy of touch, the result of long training as well as thoughtfulness, received from 11s. to 16s., and 17s. a week, whilst the roughest unskilled labour of a man was worth at least 18s."—(*Times*, March 27).

Employers alone are not to blame for the evils of underpayment. There are many just and right-minded employers who would gladly pay their work-women a fair rate of wages: but, however willing they may be to do this, they are almost powerless so long as the women themselves make no stir in the matter. If they were to pay higher wages whilst other less scrupulous employers could, without difficulty, obtain the services of women at about a third or fourth of the fair payment, they would simply be unable to carry on business, because the unscrupulous employers would be able, by paying less for labour, to undersell them in the market. Employers have been known to express their regret that they could not pay their workers better wages because those workers made no efforts in that direction.

The present isolated position of working women reacts injuriously on their prospects in many indirect, as well as direct, ways. The object of this paper is to endeavour to point out some of these evils, and to urge on the earnest attention of all concerned in the question that which the writer believes to be the only true remedy for them.

So long as women are unprotected by any kind of combination, and are consequently wholly at the mercy of employers for the rate of their wages and the length of their working hours, working men not unnaturally look with suspicion on their employment in trades in some branches of which men are engaged. The fear that the employment of women will lower their wages has led the men to pass rules in many of their trade societies positively forbidding their members to work with women.

They have also carried on, and are still continuing, an agitation, in which they are aided by many benevolent persons who desire to improve the position of women, in support of a Bill now before Parliament, to limit the hours of women's work in factories and workshops. This Bill is intended to apply also to children, with whom working women are classed, thus conveying and endeavouring to perpetuate, the idea that women are entirely unable to protect themselves, a position, to a certain extent, degraded and injurious.

Women, more than ever, urgently need the protection afforded by combination, as it is possible that, if these suggested restrictions become law, further legislation in the same direction may be proposed, and at present the women affected by it have no means of making known their collective opinion on the subject.

There can be no doubt that it is desirable, in many cases, to shorten the hours during which women work, but if this is done by legislative enactments instead of by the combined action of the workers themselves, the result may merely be the reduction of wages, already often insufficient, and sometimes complete exclusion from work, thus becoming, in place of protection, a real and grievous oppression. Where there is combined action among the workers, as in the case of men, it has been clearly seen, of late years, that no such legislation is necessary.

It is true that working men, who are joining in these well-meant but mistaken endeavours to improve the position of working women, might offer the same kind of protection which they themselves adopt. They might invite women to join their trade unions, or to assist them to form similar societies. But they do not seem to be inclined to do this. At three successive annual congresses of leaders and delegates of trades unions, the need of women's unions has been brought before them, and each time someone present has asserted that women *cannot* form unions. The only ground for this assertion appears to be that women *have not* yet formed unions. Probably they have not done so, because they have not quite seen how to set about it.

The following is an outline of a plan, in some respects similar to that of the "National Agricultural Labourers' Union", for a general organisation of working women. This organisation might ultimately be divided up into societies of different trades, but, at first, it appears desirable to make the basis of operations as general and the rules as simple as possible:

1. A central council or board, having branches composed of workers in any trade all over the country.
2. The name of the association to be the "National Protective and Benefit Union of Working Women".

119

3. A branch to consist of not less than twelve persons. Intimation of a wish to form a branch to be made to the central council, by whom the following form would be forwarded:

We, the undersigned, agree to form a branch of the "National Protective and Benefit Union of Working Women" in....
....
and we hereby appoint ....
to act as secretary, and ....
to act as treasurer to the branch.
..........18........

NAME.	ADDRESS.	TRADE

4. On the return of the form, a supply of membership forms and cards, rules and subscription books, to be sent to the person named as secretary of the branch.
5. Subscriptions to be paid to a secretary of a branch each week, and payment acknowledged in the members' subscription books. In the first instance, until district boards could be formed, the secretary of each branch should be required to forward members' payments once every month to the central council, with a list of the names and addresses of the members paying. A detailed receipt would be returned to the secretary, which she should be required to produce on application, for the satisfaction of the members.
6. The subscription to be $1\frac{1}{2}$d. per week, and the entrance fee $4\frac{1}{2}$d.
7. The entrance fees to be devoted to the working expenses of the society, including cost of printing the rules, subscription cards and forms, with which the branch members and secretaries would be supplied. Any surplus at the end of each year to be paid over to the benefit fund.
8. The subscription fees to be deposited in a bank in the name of the society, at interest, as a fund for benefit and trade purposes, by trustees appointed by the central council, whose names and position would be sufficient guarantee against fraud. The subscriptions not to be drawn upon for any working expenses. The entrance fees to be deposited

in a separate fund, and to be drawn upon by the treasurer, by written order of the central council only.

9. No member to be entitled to receive sick or out of work benefits until she has paid subscriptions for six months; the sum then granted to depend on the amount of funds accumulated.

10. Strict investigation to be made into applications for benefit payments.

It must be borne in mind that the main object in view is to accustom women to the idea of union. If this object is once gained more elaborate plans may before long be found necessary, and, as a knowledge of the strength of each trade in certain localities is arrived at, classified unions of women will be more practicable. To give an idea of the strength of working women as regard numbers, four trades may be mentioned which it may be hoped could ultimately support separate unions:

Tailoresses (number in England and Wales
    shown by Census Returns of 1871)   38,021
Earthenware manufacture   15,953
Straw plait manufacture   45,270
Bookbinders   7,557

A general union, as a commencement, would afford excellent facilities for the formation of separate unions. By the classification of the different trades of the members by the central council, it would readily be seen when a sufficient number of members of one trade were enrolled to make a union of that trade strong enough to stand alone. There are now in New York some very successful unions consisting of, and managed entirely by, working women. Two of the largest are the "Parasol and Umbrella-makers' Union", and the "Women's Typographical Union".

The advantage of a general union at the first onset are very considerable, as by its means those women who are tolerably well paid would help those who were very badly paid. If the well-paid and the ill-paid workers were to form separate unions, the ill-paid ones would be at a much greater disadvantage than if they belonged to a union having a far larger number of members than they could muster alone.

By way of encouragement, women may be reminded of what

has been done by that, until recently, worst paid and most isolated class of men, the agricultural labourers. A movement, commenced amongst them only three years ago, has already developed into a powerful society, numbering about 150,000 members. Many labourers, who were earning wages only just above starvation rates, have now increased their earnings by one third or more. If men whose circumstances were so unfavourable to combination as those of most agricultural labourers have been successful in this effort, there is every reason to hope for the success of unions of women.

There is one point with regard to the low wages of women which may here be referred to. Any remarks on this subject are often met by a reply involving a common fallacy, viz., that "all cheap production is a benefit to the producers". Does it, however, benefit women, or indeed men either, that cigars, for instance, should be made for 4d. per 100, the price paid, according to the *Beehive* newspaper, to some female cigar makers; or that the production of cartridges, in which women are largely employed, should be cheapened; or that artifical flowers should be sold at 1½d. per spray; that paper boxes for collars should be sold at so low a price that they are wasted and thrown away as of no value; or that jewel cases can be procured at a very small cost? Even in the case of articles of direct use to working women, cheap production is of but little more benefit. Wages of from 6s. to 12s. per week leave a very small margin for any purchases beyond those of the bare necessaries of life—food and fuel—and are often insufficient for a proper supply of these. Cheap production, which involves, for the producers, want, degradation, and even, occasionally, starvation; or which, when starvation is avoided, throws them upon the poor rates for maintenance, can surely not be beneficial to them or to the community.

At present only two advantages of union have been enlarged upon in this paper: the means of raising wages and of shortening hours of labour.

But were the position of working women all that could be desired with respect to both wages and hours of work, there are other benefits of union of the greatest importance. One of these is the means afforded for help in times of sickness or of temporary depression of trade. Women have suffered deeply from the want of such assistance.

APPENDIX

At a time of great slackness of trade among the bookbinders, in 1871, caused by a delay in passing through the House of Commons the revised Prayer-book, it was stated that during sixteen months two of the men's unions had paid £2500 in relieving their unemployed members, but that the women in the trade, having no union to fall back upon, had suffered the greatest distress.

The "Female Umbrella-makers Union of New York" has paid for sick benefits alone, during the three years of its existence, over 1000 dollars (£200). One member, a widow, was supported entirely by the union, during an illness lasting two years.

The union might also afford valuable aid to its members by instituting inquiries by means of the central council, into any cases of imposition or fraud which might be brought to the notice of the council. There are many gentlemen who would probably be willing to assist such an association by giving legal advice in these cases. The Working Women's Protective Union of New York has taken up this work, and frequently with great success. In the case of machine workers, employers have sometimes refused to pay for the work, under the pretence of its being badly done, and have even required the forfeiture of the workers' deposit as compensation for pretended damage to the material. The union has investigated such cases, and, where expostulation with the employer has failed, has undertaken his prosecution at law. Such frauds are now becoming every day more rare in New York, because it is now known that a powerful society is ready to protect women in this way. So long as women do not combine they are powerless under dishonest treatment, because they are well known to be too poor to follow up the defrauders.

Another service the union might render is suggested by the mention of deposits required on work. Workwomen often find it very difficult to make these advances, and the union might assist its members either by lending the deposit money, or by becoming responsible for the return of the material.

Another important advantage is the feeling of strength and mutual sympathy and helpfulness afforded by close association with others in the same position and labouring under the same difficulties as ourselves. Out of such union, too, might grow many movements for still further improving the position of women, such as some kind of co-operative work-rooms, in which women when temporarily out of employment might find means of

123

EMMA PATERSON

subsistence until they obtained permanent work; educational efforts, emigration clubs, reading-rooms, &c., &c.

The writer earnestly begs all persons interested in improving the social condition of women to communicate with her with a view to action in this matter, and especially invites information and suggestions from women engaged in trades.

EMMA A. PATERSON.
April, 1874.

Address—
MRS. PATERSON,
2, Brunswick Row,
Queen Square,
Bloomsbury, W.C.

124

Bibliography

ANDERSON, Adelaide Mary, *Women in the Factory*, E. P. Dutton (New York, 1922).

ASPINALL, A., *The Early Trade Unions*, Batchworth (London, 1949).

BESANT, Walter, *Fifty Years Ago*, Chatto and Windus (London, 1888).

BLAINEY, J., *The Woman Worker and Restrictive Legislation*, J. W. Arrowsmith (London, 1928).

BOONE, Gladys, *The Women's Trade Union League in Gt. Britain and the U.S.*, New York, Columbia University Press; P. S. King and Son (London, 1942).

BRITTAIN, Vera, *Lady into Women*, Andrew Drakers (1933).

BROWN, W. Henry, *Charles Kingsley and Parson Lot*, Co-operative Union (1924).

BRYHER, Samson, *An Account of the Labour Movement in Bristol* (1929).

BUNDOCK, Clement J., *The Story of the National Union of Printing, Bookbinding and Paper Workers*, Oxford University Press.

CARSEL, Wilfred, *A History of the Chicago Ladies' Garment Workers' Union* (Chicago, 1940).

CHECKLAND, S. G., *The Rise of Industrial Society in England, 1815–1885*, Longman's (London, 1964).

CLEGG, H. A., *General Union in a Changing Society*, Basil Blackwell (Oxford, 1964).

COLE, Margaret, *Makers of the Labour Movement*, Longmans Green (1948).

COLE, G. D. H. *British Trade Unionism in the Third Quarter of the 19th Century*, I.R.S.H. (1937).

125

COLE, G. D. H. and TILSON, A. W., *British Working Class Movements: Select Documents, 1789–1875* (London, 1951).

COMMONS, John R. and ANDREWS, J. B., *Principles of Labour Legislation* (1916).

COMMONS, John R. and associates, *History of Labour in the United States* (New York, 1918).

COMMONS and others, *Documentary History of American Industrial Society* (Cleveland, 1910–11).

DAVIS, W. J., *The British Trades Union Congress—History and Recollections*, Co-op Printing Society Ltd. (1910).

DAVIS, W. H., *History of the T.U.C.*

DILKE, Lady (E. F. S. Pattison) and WHITLEY, Margaret, *Women's Work*, Methuen (1894).

DRAKE, Barbara, *Women in Trade Unions*, Labour Research (London, 1920).

FONER, Philip, *History of Trade Unionism in America.*

FRIED, Albert and ELMAN, Richard, *Charles Booth's London*, Hutchinson (1969), Pelican Books (1971).

GREEN, Charles H., *The Headwear Workers: A Century of Trade Unionism* (New York, 1944).

HALL, B. T., *Our Fifty Years*, Working Men's Club and Institute Union (1912).

HAMILTON, Mary Agnes, *Mary Macarthur, a Biographical Sketch*, Parsons (London, 1925).

HAMILTON, Mary Agnes, *Woman at Work*, The Labour Book Service (1941).

HENRY, Alice, *The Trade Union Woman*, Appleton and Co. (1915).

HUTCHINS, B. L. and HARRISON, A., *A History of Factory Legislation*, Frank Cass (London, 1966).

HUTT, Allen, *British Trade Unionism*, Lawrence and Wishart (1941).

HUXLEY, Elspeth (compiler), *The Kingsleys, a biographical anthology*, Allen and Unwin (1973).

JENKINS, Roy, *Sir Charles Dilke*, Collins (1958).

KAMM, Josephine, *Rapiers and Battleaxes*, Allen and Unwin (London, 1966).

LEVINE, Louis, *The Women Garment Workers*, B. W. Huebsch Inc. (New York, 1924).

London Trades Council, 1866–1950, Lawrence and Wishart (1950).

MacDonald, J. Ramsay, *Women in the Printing Trades*, P. S. King and Son (Westminster, 1904).

Morton, A. L., *A People's History of England*, Gollancz (1938).

Myrdal, Alva and Klein, Viola, Routledge and Kegan Paul (London, 1956).

Oneal, James, *The Workers in American History* (New York, 1921).

Paterson, Thomas, *New Method of Mental Science*.

Pattison, E. F. S., *Trade Unions for Women* (1893).

Perlman, Selig, *A History of Trade Unionism in the United States* (New York, 1922).

Ramelson, Marian, *The Petticoat Rebellion*, Lawrence and Wishart (1967).

Roberts, C., *The Trades Union Congress, 1868–1921* (London, 1958).

Scoresby, W., *American Factories and their Female Operatives* (1845).

Strachey, Ray, *The Cause*, Bell (London, 1928).

TUC, *Women in the Trade Union Movement* (1955).

Webb, Sidney and Beatrice, *The History of Trade Unionism* (1950).

Webb, Sidney and Beatrice, *Industrial Democracy*, Longmans Green (London, 1897).

Journals

Club and Institute Journal.
Economic Journal, Vols. 1, 2 and 3.
Englishwomen's Review, December 1886.
Factories, Reports of Inspectors, 1835–1877 (semi-annually). The Annual Reports of the Chief Inspector of Factories and Workshops.
Fortnightly Review, June 1889.
Illustrated Mail (April 1, 1905).
Labour News, 1874.
TUC reports.
Women's Trade Union Review.
Women's League Journals and reports.